Stay W/

SOARING
WITH THE
EAGLES

*Patrick
I appreciate Your
friendship!*

B. Sid

SOARING
WITH THE
EAGLES

The Priority of Prayer

BLAKE GIDEON

Published by
Master Design Publishing
Fulton, Kentucky, USA

Master Design Publishing
  an imprint of Master Design Marketing, LLC
789 State Route 94 E
Fulton, KY 42041
www.masterdesign.org

Layout and Cover Design by Faithe Thomas

Printed in the USA

Dedication

Dedicated to the prayer groups of Edmond's First Baptist Church

Contents

Foreword

He had probably been watching from a distance, shifting quietly from one foot to the other, determined not to disturb his Master. Finally, at the first sign that the Lord had completed His conversation with the Father, the eager disciple could contain himself no longer. "Teach us to pray!" urged the Lord's disciple. Once again, the Lord unraveled the principles of prayer, this time noting that prayer is a definite activity, not just a theory to which His followers were to merely assent. They were "to pray!"

Countless books have been written on prayer. The book you now have in your hand is a call to the practice of prayer by someone who does it! Blake Gideon is an active pastor who practices prayer. This book is the fruit of that practice. It is not a call to endorse prayer but to enter into it. It is not a call to assent to truth but to act upon the truth you already have in hand.

Though this book may be taken as a whole and read through from cover to cover, I would urge you to stop and savor each chapter as an entity unto itself. Determine to put into practice what you have read. Let these truths make a difference in your personal practice of prayer.

To aid in your own exercise of prayer, each chapter focuses on the Biblical, historical, personal and practical aspect of its subject. Thus, the book serves not only as a doctrinal guide but as a roadmap leading to the practice of prayer.

Lest we fall into the trap of believing prayer to be mostly formal, pedantic, repetitive and ritualistic, Blake Gideon graphically reminds us that to pray is to "soar with the eagles." What a thrilling prospect! And what an adventure awaits us as we "mount up" into the divine heights through prayer.

Keep this book close at hand! You'll want to return again and again as a reminder to enroll in Christ's school of prayer—for the rest of your life!

Rejoice evermore!
Tom Elliff
2 Timothy 1:12

Introduction

"Those who hope in the Lord will renew their strength. They will soar on wings like eagles." Isaiah 40:31

Just like the flight of the eagle, prayer allows us to soar with God to heights unknown to the natural man. As a matter of fact, prayer takes us out of the natural into the supernatural. This book will introduce you to men and women who have soared with God through many trials and snares. Prayer is what allowed them to soar even in the midst of difficulty. Prayer can do the same for anyone who is truly committed to prayer.

Prayer will do more to straighten the tangled mess of people's lives than the tens of thousands of self-help books that fill the shelves of bookstores across our land. Prayer will do more to clear misunderstandings and right unhappy circumstances than all the human counselors combined. Prayer will do more to bring profound, lasting change than any prescription drug out there.

I have personally seen and experienced how prayer promotes personal piety, emotional health, and overall spiritual well-being. Yes, prayer avails mightily for others and ourselves when we are faithful to pray. Prayer is what God uses for the salvation of fallen man and the growth of the spiritual man. Furthermore, prayer will bring power into the things that we seek to do for God.

God hears prayer and grants prayer. Just typing that sentence rejoices my soul. However, I do feel the need to be a bit more specific. God hears prayer when we come to Him through Christ, and God grants prayer when it is according to His will. Prayer is not a blank check to come to God however you wish and ask for whatever you want. Prayer is a privilege for everyone who has trusted in Jesus Christ as Lord and Savior, and God takes great joy in answering prayers born from His Word.

I wrote this book to invite you, the reader, to go on a journey with me. Along the way, we will encounter Biblical prayer principles that will be life-transforming. Our guides will be men and woman of Holy Scripture, but also historical characters and personal friends.

This book is more of an eclectic compilation of essays about various elements of prayer than a systematic study of prayer. Therefore, the reader can turn to any chapter and not feel completely lost. However, I do encourage you to read each chapter in order.

Each chapter contains a reference to a passage of Scripture. I encourage you to read each passage before reading the rest of the chapter. Doing so will allow you to get the most out of this book. Not only will you be familiar with the stories being discussed, but you will see that these truths are coming directly from God's Word.

Finally, I encourage you to use this book as a personal devotional, for a small group book study, or even for sermon or lesson preparation. Because these truths are Biblical, they will have application in whatever setting you may choose.

The Family Altar

Gen. 12:1-8

There is a phrase often quoted that has become nothing more than a cliché. What is the phrase? Here it is: "A family that prays together stays together." I would like to redeem this phrase from being nothing more than a cliché to a true Biblical principle. God has ordained the family unit as a means of multiplying worshipers throughout the nations. The work of multiplication and stability is truly effective when families pray together, grow together, and stay together. It's true; broken families produce broken nations and broken nations produce a broken world. Prayer throughout the Word of God has always been the primary means for strengthening families.

Old Testament history is filled with accounts of praying men and women. The leaders of Israel in those early days were noted for their prayer habits. I want us to look at examples of a few of them so that we can see the place of prayer in their lives.

The Biblical Example: A Promised Posterity

The first Old Testament saint we will look at is Abraham. Abraham is known as the patriarch of the Jewish nation, and of the Christian faith. His life proves that prayer has always been a part of the people of God. Therefore, we can say that prayer reaches back to the early ages of man on earth. From the very beginning, Abraham had a heart for God. God called him to leave his country, his family, his place of security and comfort and go to a place that God would show him. God promised to bless him and make his name great (Gen. 12:1-2). Abraham trusted the Lord; therefore, he obeyed God. In this history of redemption, God is preparing a covenant people for Himself. He is preparing to make Israel a great nation through which the Messiah would eventually come.

However, two obstacles stood in the way before these promises could be realized in Abraham's life: Sarah's barrenness (Gen. 11:30), and the Canaanites who would seek to prevent him from settling in the land. These two obstacles stood against God's promise to make Abraham's loins fertile and his name famous.

However, take notice of how Abraham responded to the promises of God in the face of these obstacles. Genesis 12:7b-8 states, *"So he built an altar to the Lord, who had appeared to him. From there he moved to the hill country on the east of Bethel and pitched his tent, with Bethel on the west and Ai on the east. And there he built an altar to the Lord and called upon the name of the Lord."* Notice two things: he built an altar and called upon the name of the Lord. Building the altar represents consecration, while prayer represents dependence. Therefore, worship for the patriarchs was composed of both action (building the altar) and prayer (invoking the name of God). Building the altar was a figurative way of claiming the land for God. In the same way, we are to pray around our family altars and claim all we have for the glory of God.

We learn from the Scriptures that this was an activity the patriarchs often engaged in (Gen. 12:8, 13:18, 22:9, 26:25, 33:20, 35:7). Building the altar was associated with invoking the name of Yahweh.[1] It is also worth noting that while the tents were dismantled, the altars always stood.

When Abraham built the altar, he was primarily doing two things: dedicating the land to the Lord, and more importantly, dedicating his family to the Lord. The family altar was very important to Abraham, and as a result of his example, the family altar became important to the generations that followed him.

Sadly, the family altar is something that is mostly forgotten or at least neglected in today's modern Christian households. The altar must be restored and never torn down. The primary responsibility of erecting the altar lies squarely on the shoulders of fathers. However, if the father is absent, then the mother must see to it that the family altar is honored in her home.

The family altar will alter you.

---

[1] Victor Hamilton, *The New International Commentary on the Old Testament: The Book of Genesis, Chapters 1-17* (Grand Rapids: William B. Eerdmans Publishing Co, 1990), 378.

The Theological Example: The Reaching Power of Prayer

In his classic book entitled, *The Doctrine of Prayer*, T.W. Hunt makes the following statement, "Prayer is universal throughout time. Throughout the Bible and throughout the ages, prayer has sustained the people of God." Hunt further wrote on the universal nature of prayer in regard to space. Prayer knows no geographical, racial, or ethnic lines. Prayer pervades not only our present but also our future. Let me further explain. God is omnipresent, which means He is all present everywhere. He is in all dimensions, in all times, and in all places. He works in time, but He is also transcendent, which means, He is outside of space and time. What are the implications of such truth? If I pray to God today (in the present), it has the potential to affect the future since God is already there. He is not limited to time like we are. Furthermore, if I pray to God while living in Oklahoma, it has the power to be used by God to affect someone on the other side of the world, since God is not limited to space. Both truths are further explained using the following example: I am praying for spiritual awakening to invade America. However, I may not see awakening in my lifetime, but let's say, long after I'm gone, spiritual awakening does come to America. Did my prayers, which were lifted to God in the past, play a part? Absolutely they did! Can we say this about anything else? The answer is no! There is nothing more powerful than prayer.

"When the revival in Wales was at its height, a Welsh missionary wrote home begging the people to pray that India might be moved in like manner. So the coal miners met daily at the mouth of the mine half an hour before dawn to pray for their comrades overseas, soon the blessings of revival hit India. Isn't it just amazing to know that by our prayers we can bring down showers of blessings upon India, or Africa, or China?"[2]

My mother prayed for me when I was just an infant. She prayed that God would use me as a preacher of the gospel. After many years of living a life of rebellion against God, He granted my mother's prayer. He saved me and called me into ministry at the age of 24. The prayer she prayed twenty-four years earlier affected my future. Think about it, all revivals throughout church history have been the results of prayer. Many things we do amount to nothing, but the prayers we pray will never be lost. Prayer has the power to change today, affect tomorrow, and to reach around the world to change lives. One day we will die, but the prayers we pray will never die.

Rest assured, the gauge of your family's influence in the world is not the size of your bank account, or the degrees hanging on the wall, but the earnestness of your prayers. Little prayer results in little influence. Think about it; every conversion is the results of someone's prayers. God will do more through our prayers than He will through anything else. Often, we hear people say, "all I can do is pray," thus, treating prayer like a last resort. To the contrary, prayer is the best thing we can do. Prayer is the key to unlocking God's storehouse of blessings. I love what E.M. Bounds writes in regard to prayer and the promises of God, "Prayer as a spiritual energy, and illustrated in its enlarged and mighty working, makes way for and brings into practical realization the promises of God."[3] During your family

---

[2] Albert Ernest Richardson, *The Kneeling Christian* (Alachua, Fla: Bridges Logos Foundation, 2007), 29.

[3] E.M. Bounds, *The Possibilities of Prayer* (Grand Rapids: Baker

altar time, take hold of the promises of God and pray accordingly. Charles Spurgeon encouraged this truth in the following words:

> Beloved brethren and sisters in Christ, let us learn from our Savior's example to plead the promises of God when we go to him in prayer. Praying without a promise is like going to war without a weapon. God is so gracious that he may yield to our entreaties even when he has not given a definite promise concerning what we are asking at his hands, but going to him with one of his own promises is like going to a bank with a check: he must honor his own promises. We speak reverently, yet very confidently, upon this point. To be consistent with his own character, he must fulfill his own word which he has spoken; so, when you approach the throne of grace, search out the promise that applies to your case, and plead it with your heavenly Father, and then expect that he will do as he has said.[4]

We also learn from prayer that God is very personal in how He deals with people. God is seeking to have fellowship with people who have a heart like His. The fact that God desires fellowship says a lot about His own personhood. Our fellowship with God grows in intimacy as we pray. We are drawn closer to God as we pray. Furthermore, when you pray with your family around the family altar, not only will you grow in personal intimacy with God, but you will grow

---

Book House, 1979), 17.

    [4] Charles Spurgeon, *The Prayers of Christ* (Peabody Mass: Hendrickson Publishers, 2014), 4.

in intimacy with your family as well, and your family will grow in intimacy with God. I often tell people, prayer is one of the most intimate things we can do. Think about the personhood of God and His promises in light of this verse, *"You make known to me the path of life; in your presence there is fullness of joy; at your right hand are pleasure forevermore"* (Ps. 16:11). Therefore, we see the personhood of God in the fact that He has decreed the prayers of believers as the means of accomplishing His divine purposes around the world.

The family altar will alter your perspective.

The Historical Example: A Mother Devoted to Prayer

John Wesley was one of the greatest evangelists of the 1700s. God used John Wesley mightily. He preached the gospel to thousands of people. He was one of the small flames that God used to set ablaze the first Great Awakening in British and American history.

"Wesley was driven by the conviction that as long as he had breath this side of eternity, he would spend his life sharing the gospel. He covered nearly 250,000 miles, mostly horseback. He preached over 40,000 sermons and wrote approximately 250 books and tracts. He sought the most opportune place in each town he visited. He used squares, the marketplace, hillsides, any place that would help the message be heard."[5]

Charles Wesley was the brother of John. He wrote over 9,000 hymns, many that we still sing today. He is also

---

[5] Malcolm McDow & Alvin Reid, *Firefall: How God Has Shaped History Through Revivals* (Nashville: B&H Publishing, 1997), 194.

known as one of the most prolific Christian poets. Together, these two men have made an indelible impact on Christianity as we know it today. However, the story of these two men started way before the 1st Great Awakening. You see, when these two men were just infants, their mother, Susannah, prayed for them and their other siblings. She was a remarkable woman. "She taught each of her children personally. Although thirteen of her children died at a young age, illustrating the high infant mortality rate, two of those reached adulthood (John and Charles). Their family life included morning and evening devotions accompanied by prayer. She would also devote time with each child to discuss spiritual matters."[6] There were times when she would pull her apron up over her head, while the children play at her feet, just to have some time alone with the Lord. For both she and her father, Dr. Samuel Annesley, guarding the family altar was essential.

The family altar will alter your family.

The Personal Example: Prayer's Priority in Marriage

In my home, the kitchen table serves as the altar for my family. Of course, we are not offering physical animal sacrifices, Christ is the ultimate sacrifice, and He died once for all. Instead, we sit together, have our meal together, and then together, we actively engage God in Bible study and prayer. This is my way of continually dedicating my home and my family to the service of the Lord. Altars, for Abraham, were essentially a place to gather his household together for family worship. This is to be distinguished from his personal secret prayer time with God.

---

[6] Ibid., 186.

I also have an altar dedicated for just Kelly (my wife) and me. The second altar is in our bedroom; yes, it's our bed. Stop! It is not what you're thinking. Every morning we wake up together around six o'clock. Kelly is the morning person, so she has the coffee ready. During this time, we spend about thirty minutes reading the Bible together (usually through a daily Bible reading plan) and we pray together. This is a very special time for us. We realize that we need God to be first if our marriage is going to continue thriving.

Kelly and I are not perfect, and we know our kids are not perfect, but we are doing our best to set our family up for spiritual success. We desire to raise children who love and fear God. We want them to understand the importance of both devotion and discipline. Prayer is absolutely essential. Therefore, we are seeking to make prayer a priority.

Recently, during our own family altar time, we prayed for my sister-in-law who had been struggling with cancer. Her original diagnosis was not good. Immediately, many began to pray for her, including my family. Each night we gathered around our family altar (the kitchen table) with the Bible in hand, and we prayed fervently for her healing. God graciously heard our prayers and the prayers of many others, which resulted in my sister-in-law's healing. What a blessing to know that God has chosen to use our prayers as a means of accomplishing His divine purposes.

The family altar time will alter your marriage.

"Prayer is a wonderful power placed by Almighty God in the hands of His saints, which may be used to accomplish great purposes and to achieve unusual results." — E.M. Bounds

Practical Advice

1. Decide a time in the day to have your family altar time.

2. Dedicate a place in your home for family altar time.

3. Discipline yourself to guard the family altar time.

Encouragement

We are all busy people. Often life becomes overwhelming, and there will be days when the family altar time will be pushed out by other things. When this happens, please don't condemn yourself. Remember, this is about love, not legalism. Just start back where you left off. However, be sure to guard yourself against setting a pattern of persistent neglect.

The Power of Intercession

Exodus 32

Have you ever prayed and wondered if prayer even works? Some of you have prayed for children who are away from the Lord. Others have prayed for your marriage. Still, others have prayed for healing. What are we to do when we pray, and it seems like nothing happens? Should we give up on prayer? Sadly, for many, this is exactly what happens. They become impatient and as a result, stop praying.

Furthermore, there is the issue of God's promises and His wrath. The promises of God are sure, but so is His wrath. There are certain times in Scripture when the wrath of God seems to threaten His promises. Such is the case concerning Israel at Sinai. For example, God promised to lead the nation of Israel out of Egyptian bondage, which He did, and take them back to the land of promise. However, after the Israelites crossed the Red Sea, and consecrated themselves at Sinai, God threatened to destroy them. Why would the God of promise make such a threat? How should we respond to this and what effect does it have on our prayer lives? Let's take a closer look at Exodus 32.

The Biblical Look: The Wrath of God Withheld

The chapter begins with a brief statement regarding the delay of Moses to come down off the mountain. It's here that we find the event that threatens God's promise. Moses was away; Aaron was in charge; and the people were impatient. The people plead with Aaron to make them gods "who shall go before them." Aaron gave into the desires of the people.

Concerning this event, Peter Enns writes, "Aaron fashions a calf out of gold, and the Israelites proclaim it to be the god that brought them out of Egypt. This amounts to an attempt to undo what has just taken place in the preceding thirty-one chapters: the Exodus, the covenant, and the initiation of God's presence in the tabernacle. In this brief but horrifying moment, God almost gives them what they seem to want, were it not for Moses' intercession."[7]

Their act was nothing more than blatant rebellion—an attempt to remove God from His rightful place. The choice of a calf was not by happenstance. The calf/bull was a common deity in the ancient world. As a matter of fact, the Egyptian fertility god (Apis) was portrayed as a bull. Further, it was probably no arbitrary decision to make the

---

[7] Peter Enns, *The NIV Application Commentary: Exodus* (Grand Rapids: Zondervan, 2000), 568.

calf covered in gold since they wanted it to stand in the place of the tabernacle, which represented God's continual presence among His people.

As stated above, Apis was the fertility god of the Egyptians. Therefore, the worship of Apis was characterized by orgies and other acts of sexual immorality. Here we see the Israelites engaging in the pagan practices of the Egyptians. The depravity of the Israelites caused the righteous indignation of God to be revealed. His anger was fierce against the idolatry of His chosen people. God was prepared to destroy the people and start over with Moses. Obviously, this is reminiscent of God's act of destruction in the days of Noah.

However, Moses immediately interceded on behalf of the rebellious people. What does it mean to "intercede?" Let me borrow a quote from Oswald Chambers; he writes, "People describe intercession by saying, 'it is putting yourself in someone else's place.' That is not true! Intercession is putting yourself in God's place; it is having His mind and His perspective." I truly believe this is the very thing we see Moses doing here. Moses, whose very life beats with the heart of God, expresses mercy for the people. In all actuality, it is the heart of God in Moses that expresses mercy through intercession on behalf of the rebellious people. Remember, Moses served as God's representative. God knew in advance that He would use the intercessory prayer of Moses to accomplish what His hand had already preordained. Thus, God used the prayer of Moses to accomplish His divine purpose.

The intercessory prayer of Moses itself was a part of God's foreordained plan to show grace. However, from man's perspective it seems as though God "relented," or as some translations state, "God changed His mind." This phrase is known as an *anthropomorphism*. This is when human traits or emotions are used to describe God. To say "God changed His mind" seems to suggest that God did not know in advance what He was going to do. Therefore, I believe the best translation is "relent." God knew in advance He would not destroy the people, but He chose to use the intercessory prayer of Moses to accomplish His act of mercy. They go hand-in-hand. In the words of E.M. Bounds, "Israel as a nation would have met their just destruction and their just fate after their apostasy with the golden calf had it not been for the intercession of Moses' forty days' and forty nights' praying."[8]

Therefore, because God chose the means of accomplishing His purpose (prayer), we can say that is was the intercessory prayer of Moses that stayed the hand of God. God has also chosen to use our prayers as the means of accomplishing His divine purposes. Make no mistake about it; there is power in intercessory prayer because God has ordained it. It was E.M. Bounds who stated, "Prayer influences God greatly." All one has to do is recall the intercessory prayer of Abraham on behalf of Sodom and Gomorrah. God had doomed the wicked city of Sodom, the residence of Abraham's nephew Lot. However, the fate of Sodom was stayed for a while as the direct result of Abraham's intercessory prayer. Nothing would save Sodom but prayer, so Abraham prayed. Ultimately, Sodom was doomed, but we only wonder if things would have been different if Abraham would have kept praying. His optimism for the wicked city led him to cut short his prayers. Let us not cut

---

[8] E.M. Bounds, *Prayer And Praying Men* (Grand Rapids, Baker Book House, 1977), 33.

short our intercession; plead with God for the salvation of the lost. Remember, your unceasing merciful intercession is a reflection of His heart.

Concerning Moses' intercessory prayer, there is something worth noting. Moses' intercessory prayer was only partly successful. God did not reject His people as a whole, but sinful individuals were judged. That day three thousand people died as a result of God's righteous indignation. The limitation of Moses' intercessory prayer serves as a pointer and a reminder that we all need a greater intercessor that will provide complete atonement for the people. That greater intercessor is Jesus.

The Theological Look: A Divine Mystery

We see the power of intercessory prayer at work in regard to Moses' prayer for Israel. In this section, I will discuss the theological mystery of intercessory prayer as it relates to the providence of God. Let me begin by saying that the promises of God find their fulfillment in prayer and this is according to His divine providence. The Westminster Confession of Faith defines "providence" as follows: "God, the Creator of all things, doth uphold, direct dispose, and governs all creatures, actions, and things, from the greatest even to the least, by His most wise and holy providence, according to His infallible foreknowledge, and the free and immutable counsel of His own will to the praise of the glory of His wisdom, power, justice, goodness, and mercy." A frequent objection raised by many concerning the doctrine of God's providence is that such teaching renders prayer useless. Their logic goes something like this, "If God governs all things, then how can man be responsible for his actions, and what need is there then for prayer when

God ordains what will be?" Of course, this is a very logical argument, but it's only unanswerable if we choose to rely wholly on human reason. However, we must admit, there are limits to human understanding. God is infinite, but we are finite.

When we realize the Bible affirms both the providence of God and prayer, then we must too. Many arguments are based on a misunderstanding of prayer. There are Christians who assume we pray to change God's mind. However, this could not be further from the truth. J.I. Packer writes the following concerning prayer: "The prayer of a Christian is not an attempt to force God's hand, but a humble acknowledgment of helplessness and dependence."[9] Concerning Moses, this is exactly what we learn in our passage. Moses prayed to God because he realized he was utterly helpless to change the situation. He cried to God in dependence, and this is where God wanted him to be spiritually. Prayer is not about changing God; it's about God changing us.

It is true that our prayers cannot change God's eternal decrees, but we do know He uses prayer to accomplish them. Moses is a great example. Obviously, it was part of God's eternal decree not to destroy Israel completely, and He used prayer to accomplish His purpose. The logical question is, "What if Moses had not prayed, is it possible that God would have destroyed the people completely?" This is a question we simply cannot answer. The secret things are to be left to the Lord (Deut. 29:29). Here we find a divine mystery and our job is to let the mystery

---

[9] J.I. Packer, *Evangelism And The Sovereignty Of God* (Downers Grove: IVP Books, 1961), 15.

remain, not rationalize it away with limited human logic. All we know is that God is sovereign, and we are to pray.

However, we do learn from Scripture that in some sense prayer does change things. For example, we read in James 5:16-18, *"Therefore, confess your sins to one another and pray for one another, that you may be healed. The prayer of a righteous person has great powers as it is working. Elijah was a man with a nature like ours, and he prayed fervently that it might not rain and for three years and six months it did not rain on the earth. Then he prayed again and heaven gave rain and earth bore its fruit"* (ESV translation). James offers Elijah as an example of the power of intercessory prayer, and clearly, Elijah's prayer brought change. Perhaps, some would say, "Everything Elijah prayed for was already decreed by God and would have happened anyway." Even though this may be true, this type of logic only serves to downplay the importance of prayer. However, this is not how it is portrayed in this passage. The passage points to the fact that Elijah's prayer moved the hand of God to accomplish His divine purpose. Of course, God does not need us, but He has chosen to use us. God is not bound unless we pray, but prayer does move God. Once again, let the mystery remain, and pray fervently. I would like to share with you one of the most convicting paragraphs I have ever read in a book.

Do you ask, 'Well now, where do we go from here?' The answer is, 'Where sinful individuals or sinful nations can only go—back to a merciful God.' Hear me! Every church without a prayer meeting condemns us; every Bible daily unopened condemns us; every promise of

God unused condemns us; every lost neighbor condemns us; every lost heathen condemns us; every dry eye among us condemns us; every wasted minute of our time condemns us; every unclaimed opportunity of God condemns us. Next year is not ours. Tomorrow may be too late. Unless we repent, unless we return and fire the prayer altars now, unless we fast and weep now, woe unto us at the judgment...

The preceding paragraph was written by one of the great revivalist, Leonard Ravenhill, in his book, *Revival Praying*. This should be our response to the providence of God. The reality of God's providence and sovereignty does not promote laziness in regard to praying. To the contrary, such grace should drive us to our knees in dependence upon God in prayer.

It is not for us to know God's eternal decrees, but we do know He uses prayer to accomplish them. Once again, God in His divine providence has chosen *to uphold all things, direct, dispose and, govern all things* through the prayers of His righteous people. True fervent prayer does accomplish much. Therefore, the reality of God's divine providence should not hinder praying, but instead, it should motivate praying.

I will share some final thoughts on the subject of prayer and divine providence. In Matt. 24:14, Jesus states, "And the gospel of the kingdom will be proclaimed throughout the whole world as a testimony to all nations, and then the end will come." Jesus, according to divine providence, stated that the gospel would be proclaimed to the whole world. However, in Luke 10:2, Jesus commanded, "The harvest is plentiful, but the laborers are few. Therefore pray earnestly to the Lord of the harvest to send out laborers into His harvest." Therefore, the means of accomplishing Matt. 24:14, is Luke 10:2. The gospel will be proclaimed as we earnestly pray for laborers. Therefore, the means cannot be separated from the end.

We are free moral agents, who have a will. More often than we would like to admit, we exercise our will outside of the will of God. However, the more we grow in grace and prayer, the more deeply our daily lives will move in regard to God's providence. Therefore, when interceding for others, we should pray that their will will be conformed to God's. Once again, let the mystery of prayer and divine providence remain. Don't try to rationalize it away using human logic.

Personally, I have resolved to uphold the providence of God in my praying, realizing everything is dependent upon Him. But, I will pray with fervency as if everything is dependent on me, and at the end of my praying, I will rest in Him knowing that He is sovereign. I believe this is the same attitude E.M. Bounds had when he wrote these words:

> The progress to consummation of God's work in this world has two basic principles—God's ability to give and man's ability to ask. Failure in either one is fatal to the success of God's work on earth. God's inability to do or to give would put an end to redemption. Man's failure to pray would, just as surely, set a limit to the plan. But God's ability to do and to give has never failed and cannot fail, but man's ability to ask can fail and often does. Therefore, the

slow progress which is being made toward the realization of a world won for Christ lies entirely with man's limited asking. There is need for the entire Church of God on the earth to betake itself to prayer. The Church upon its knees would bring heaven upon the earth.[10]

The Historical Look: The Cost of Revival

John Hyde (1865-1912) was an American missionary from Illinois. He came to believe that God was calling him to India. He departed for India in 1892 to preach in the Punjab region. He was an extraordinary man of prayer who became known as "Praying Hyde." As he was partially deaf, he struggled to learn the native languages. Also, while in India, he continued to focus his study mostly on Scripture. His mission at first gained few converts, and he faced persecution, so he began to pray very intensely. From 1899 he began to spend entire nights in prayer to God. He would spend hours and hours with his Lord, forgetting about sleep and food, praying for believers and the unsaved. He would often pray, "Oh God, give me souls or I die!" This would become one of his most famous prayers.[11]

After a time of fruitlessness on the mission field, the Lord started moving in John's heart to pray for one soul a day to be saved. His prayer for one soul resulted in more than four hundred being gathered into God's kingdom that year. Ultimately, he gave way to praying for two people a day to

---

[10] E.M. Bounds, *The Weapon of Prayer* (Grand Rapids: Baker Book House, 1931), 57.

[11] Information gathered from the book *Praying Hyde* by Francis McGraw (Minneapolis: Bethany Fellowship, 1970).

be saved and by the end of that year, eight hundred souls were gathered into the kingdom. However, this did not satisfy his longing. Therefore, he started praying for four souls a day to be saved.[12] John Hyde was a man of great intercession. He seemed always to be hearing Jesus' voice saying, "other sheep I have, other sheep I have." No matter if he won one a day, two a day or four a day, he had an unsatisfied longing. Here is a picture given by one of his friends from India.

> As a personal worker, he would engage a man in a talk about his salvation. By and by he would have his hands on the man's shoulders, be looking him very earnestly in the eye. Soon he would get the man on his knees, confessing sins and seeking salvation. Such a one he would baptize in the village, by the roadside, or anywhere.[13]

John Hyde started the Sialkot Conventions in 1904. Through these meetings, God's revival power would touch many missionaries and change thousands of indigenous people's lives forever. Before each year's convention, John spent long nights in prayer to God. God blessed the intercessory prayers of John Hyde. However, revival did not come without a cost. It meant long journeys, late nights of staying awake and diligent in prayer, fasting, pain, and conflict. He missed many meals, and when people went to his room, they would find him in soul travail, praying earnestly for the lost. Intercessory prayer for the lost burned within his bones. He saw this as a burden he must carry. God heard the fervent intercessory prayers of John Hyde

[12] Ibid., 44.
[13] Ibid., 46.

and blessed him abundantly with many indigenous people being won to the Lord.

When John Hyde died in 1912, his body bearing the marks of his life of prayer, his last words were: "Shout the victory of Jesus Christ." He was one of the most successful Christian missionaries ever to step foot in India. Primarily, this was due to his unceasing intercession and evangelism. Oh, how we need more intercessors like Praying Hyde in our day.

The Personal Look: A Wayward Relative

Soon after my own salvation experience, I started praying for the salvation of one of my closest relatives. His heart was hard and given over to the world. There were times when I thought, "What is the point of praying? He only seems to be getting worse." However, I knew prayer is what God wanted me to do, so out of love for God and my relative, I continued to pray. I interceded to God on his behalf. I pleaded with God to break his heart and bring him to salvation. As time went on, I continued to think, "Is he ever going to be saved?"

One Sunday morning while nearing the end of my sermon, I saw the back door of the church open wide, and there in the doorway stood my relative. He immediately started walking the aisle toward me as I continued preaching. As he got closer, I could tell he was not going to stop until he got to me. I stopped preaching and met him at the altar where he gave his heart to Christ. The next Sunday I was privileged to baptize him.

Just writing this testimony fills my heart with so much joy. Never underestimate the power of intercession.

Application

1. Make a prayer list.

2. Pray over the names on the list daily.

3. Ask God to use you as an answer to the prayer.

The School of Prayer

1 Kings 17:1-24; 18:17-40

As we have already established, prayer is of the utmost importance in a believer's life. Without prayer, we simply cannot please God. Having our prayer lives deepened is not an easy task. God will bring trials in our lives for the very purpose of drawing us closer to Him and strengthening our prayer lives.

The Biblical Look: A Praying Prophet

The man named Elijah appears on the scene without any formal announcement. The name Elijah literally means "Yahweh is God." He is presented as one of the great prophets of God. The power of his prayer life is put on display. For example, he prayed for drought, and in response God sent drought. He also prayed for a poor widow's son to be raised from the dead. God heard his prayers and raised the boy from the dead. On another occasion, he prayed for rain, and God sent rain from heaven. However, despite the power of his prayer life, he is not displayed as a superhuman. To the contrary, he is portrayed as a very human figure. There are times in his life when he becomes afraid and discouraged. He is just like you and me, but his prayers are powerful. I don't know about you, but I would like for my prayers to be as powerful as his. Elijah is an example worth modeling. Christians who pray like Elijah are the great need of our day. However, to pray like Elijah, you and I must be willing to enroll in the school of prayer. It is important to note before moving on that God is the main character in this narrative, not Elijah. Therefore, what is it that we learn about God from these passages?

The theme of these passages is the struggle between Yahwism and Baalism. Therefore, it is important that we begin with a basic understanding of Baalism. Baalism existed as a religion of several centuries in various ancient Near Eastern countries. The Baalism practiced by Ahab and Jezebel saw Baal as the storm-god. Thus, Baal worshipers believed that their god made the rain. For this reason, Elijah prayed for a drought to prove that Yahweh, not Baal, is the true God in charge of the rains.[14]

In times of drought, Baal leaders would explain that Baal submitted to the false god Mot, the god of death, each year, causing drought and barrenness. Eventually, the false god, Anat, would allegedly defeat Mot and free Baal from death. Thus, by the continuation of the drought in this passage,

---

[14] Paul R. House, *The New American Commentary: 1, 2 Kings* (Nashville: B&H Publishing, 1995), 210.

the narrator exposes Baal as a false god while establishing the sovereignty of Yahweh (the covenant God of Israel). Jezebel, the wicked wife of Ahab, desired the destruction of Yahwism. She wanted it replaced with Baalism. However, Yahweh had other plans, and he used Elijah to accomplish them. But first, Elijah had to be enrolled in the school of prayer.[15]

First, God placed Elijah in a lonely place (17:1-7). God placed Elijah in a place of solitude to teach him an invaluable lesson. Faith is key to praying effectively. I would be so bold as to say that prayer without faith is not prayer at all. God placed Elijah in this lonely place to strengthen his faith, which in turn, had a positive impact on his prayer. Here we see that regardless of the harsh physical conditions, God provides for His prophet. As Elijah learned of God's provision in the lonely place, his faith and prayers were strengthened. "Nothing he needs has been withheld, a point that must be recalled for the future."[16] God was preparing His prophet for something greater.

Second, God placed him in a hard place (17:8-24). Up to this point, God has shown Elijah His faithfulness to provide. However, the problems faced by Elijah only grew in difficulty and intensity. In our previous narrative, God instructed Elijah to leave the brook that had "dried up" only to enter a more difficult situation. God instructed him to go to Zarephath, which is the heartland of Baal worship. It's here that God intended to beat Baal in his own territory. Remember, the sign of drought meant that Baal was dead and could not raise the widow's son. However,

---

[15] Ibid., 211.
[16] Ibid., 213.

Yahweh is the living God. "Elijah's faith in the midst of uncertainty allows God to use him to demonstrate His life-giving power, His constant watchfulness, and His compassion even on those outside the elect nation."[17] This raises the question, "If this is true for pagans, how much more so for the people of God?" Ultimately, God demonstrated His great power by raising the widow's son from the dead. Once again, Elijah's faith is strengthened as he learns of God's power in the hard place. As his faith was strengthened, his prayers became more effective.

Third, God placed him in a dangerous place (18:17-40). Strong faith was absolutely essential for the next task God was calling Elijah to; this one would prove to be the most difficult. Here we find Elijah face-to-face with the man who wanted him dead. Ahab blamed Elijah for the drought, but oddly enough, he did not have him immediately killed. Once again, we see that God is in control of the events in Elijah's life. Elijah suggested a contest to determine who the true God is, Yahweh or Baal. The site chosen was Mt. Carmel.

Ahab agreed to the terms and apparently believed the odds were in his favor. Ultimately, he believed the contest would rid him of the pesky prophet. The contest would be held around an altar, which the true God would consume with fire. The prophets of Baal interceded fervently to their god, but to no avail. After a few chide remarks, Elijah built the altar. He had it soaked with water to remove all doubt of the miracle that was about to occur. Elijah prayed that the name of Yahweh would be vindicated, and fire fell from heaven and consumed the altar. The observant people saw

---

[17] Ibid., 215.

the uselessness of Baal, and for a moment, became strict worshipers of Yahweh.

Without a doubt, we see that God had Elijah in the lonely place to teach him about His provision, and God had Elijah in the hard place to teach him about His power. Finally, God had him in the dangerous place to teach him about His purpose, which was to make His name known. God took Elijah through the school of prayer to prepare him for something great, which ultimately was not about him, but God.

The Theological Look: The Necessity of Faith

Here, I intend to answer the question, "What place does faith play in prayer?" Regarding this question, a few verses immediately come to mind. First is Hebrews 11:6, which states, *"And without faith it is impossible to please Him, for whoever would draw near to God must believe that He exists and that He rewards those who seek Him."* Here, we learn a spiritual truth that concerns the life of every believer. Simon J. Kistemaker writes the following concerning this passage.

> In one beautifully constructed verse, the writer of Hebrews communicates the method of pleasing God. The word "impossible" conveys the idea that faith is the indispensable ingredient for pleasing Him. When the believer prays to God, he must believe that God exists. Although God's existence is an established truth for the believer, repeatedly he will ignore God by failing to pray to Him. God however, desires

that all believers pray to Him continually in faith.[18]

Therefore, when praying to God, the believer must seek to banish doubt from every corner of his or her heart. We must pray according to the promises of God while trusting Him to fulfill such promises. It was the Apostle James who wrote, *"If any of you lacks wisdom, let him ask of God, who gives generously to all without reproach, and it will be given him. But let him ask in faith, with no doubting, for the one who doubts is like a wave of the sea that is driven and tossed by the wind. For that person must not suppose that he will receive anything from the Lord; he is double-minded, unstable in all his ways"* (James 1:5-8). James regards doubting as questioning the very character of God. When a believer prays according to the promises of God, he or she should trust God to be faithful to His promises. Remember, it is the very character of God to provide for His children.

Furthermore, James depicts the doubter as someone who is unwilling to take a stand on the promises of God. Thus, the doubter is compared to a "wave" or billow in the sea that is blown by the wind and tossed back and forth. A wave is always shifting and is never solid, never sure where or what it is, without foundation.[19] So it is of a person who prays without faith. Prayer offered up to God without faith is useless. The same can be said about faith, "Faith that ceases to pray, ceases to live."[20] A prayer of faith realizes

[18] William Hendriksen and Simon J. Kistenmaker, *New Testament Commentary: Thessalonians, the Pastorals, and Hebrews* (Grand Rapids: Baker Academic, 1984), 317.

[19] Dan G. McCartney, *Baker Exegetical Commentary On The New Testament: James* (Grand Rapids: Baker Academic, 2009), 90.

[20] E.M. Bounds, *The Necessity Of Prayer* (Grand Rapids: Baker

that nothing is impossible for God. Faith will soon become disheartened if it is not cultivated in an atmosphere of prayer. It was E.M. Bounds who wrote, "Faith trusts God today, and dispels all fears for tomorrow. Faith brings great ease of mind and perfect peace of heart."[21] No wonder the enemy loves nothing more than to tempt us not to pray, for faith grows in the school of prayer. As seen above, the school of prayer can be lonely, hard, and dangerous, but the goal of increasing our faith is worth it all, especially if we want ease of mind and peace of heart.

Faith that is truly faith must be acted upon. I must take hold of the promises of God as if I have already received them. This is what it means to pray in faith. The author of Hebrews tells us, *"Now faith is the assurance of things hoped for, the conviction of things not seen"* (Hebrews 11:1). Notice that faith is having the unwavering confidence in what we hope for. Let me explain. If I already have possession of something that was once only a promise, I will have certainty in my heart. But what if I don't already have possession of what is promised? Will I still have the same confidence? According to the Scripture, the answer should be, "yes!" Therefore, I may not currently have possession of a promise from God, but I am to live as if I already have possession of it. This is the inner conviction that the things I am unable to see are real.[22] Thus, I am to pray with conviction concerning the promises of God, believing that God will do what He said He would do. After all, "Faith is not an aimless act of the soul, but a looking to God and a resting in His promises."[23] Prayer is the primary avenue

---

Book House, 1976), 10.

[21] Ibid., 17.

[22] Kistemaker, 311.

[23] Bounds, 22.

upon which we rest upon these promises. Thus, prayer and faith are never to be separated. Prayer is the hand that fits within the glove of faith. Prayer puts my faith to work, but also, my faith gives birth to my prayers.

But one may ask, "what if the promise is delayed?" Delayed promises are tests in the classroom of the school of prayer. Remember, God is always teaching us something about His character. E.M. Bounds writes, "Delay is often the test and the strength of faith. How much patience is required when these times of testing come? Yet, faith gathers strength by waiting and praying. Patience has its perfect work in the school of delay."[24] Therefore, delay teaches us patience, which in turn strengthens our faith. We learn that God is faithful even in the midst of delay. Let me conclude this portion by quoting from E.M. Bounds once again, "Faith grows by reading and meditating upon the Word of God. Most, and best of all, faith thrives in an atmosphere of prayer."[25]

The Historical Look: A Life Marked by Prayer

The following excerpts are taken from John Piper's book, *The Hidden Smile of God: The Fruit of Affliction in the Lives of John Bunyan, William Cowper, and David Brainerd.*

David Brainerd was born on April 20, 1718, in Haddam Connecticut. Brainerd's father, Hezekiah, was a Connecticut legislator. He died when David was nine years old. Brainerd was the sixth child and third son born to Hezekiah and Dorothy. After him came three more children. Dorothy had brought one little boy from a

---

[24] Ibid., 15.
[25] Ibid., 26.

previous marriage, so there were twelve in the home—but not for long. Five years after his father died at the age of forty-six, David's mother died just before he turned fourteen.

It seems there was an unusual strain of weakness and depression in the family. Not only did the parents die early, but also, David's brother Nehemiah died at thirty-two, his brother Israel died at twenty-three, his sister Jerusha died at thirty-four, and he died at twenty-nine. As a result of such loss, David battled with depression for years.

For years, Brainerd rebelled against God. He did not like the idea that there was nothing he could do in his own strength to commend himself to God. But one day a miracle occurred. Half an hour before sunset at the age of twenty-one, he was in a lonely place praying. He wrote the following concerning the event: "Thus, the Lord I trust, brought me to a hearty desire to exalt Him, to set Him on the throne and to seek first His kingdom." He had been converted.

Two months later, he entered Yale to prepare for ministry. However, within a year he was sent home because he was too sick to study. So even at this early age, he had already contracted the tuberculosis he would die from seven years later. When he came back to Yale in 1740, he rose to the top of his class academically but was eventually expelled in 1742 during his third year. He was overheard accusing one of the professors of being lost.

Later, Brainerd would be appointed as a missionary to the Indians. He arrived on April 1, 1743, and preached for one year, using an interpreter and trying to learn the language.

Throughout his short but effective ministry, he struggled with constant sickness. In August 1746, he wrote in his diary, "Having lain in cold sweat all night, I coughed much bloody matter this morning and was under great disorder of body, and not a little melancholy" (pg. 240). Yet, he pressed on in his work.

Brainerd also struggled with recurring depression. At times he was immobilized by distresses and couldn't function. However, it is simply amazing how he pressed on in the midst of such affliction of body and soul. Brainerd also struggled with loneliness; he remained alone in ministry until the end. He also struggled with external hardships. Frequently, he would get lost in the wilderness and spend the night cold and wet. However, he writes, "Such fatigues and hardships serve to wean me more and more from the earth and trust it will make heaven sweeter" (pg. 274).

In the midst of the difficulties and struggles, Brainerd remained true to his calling. He was driven by a desire to finish well. What was most remarkable about Brainerd was his prayer life. Daily, he laid hold of the promises of God in faith, which enabled him to press on and be used by God mightily. He had a short life and a short ministry but it affected the lives of men that God has used to change the world. Such men are the likes of Johnathan Edwards, John Wesley, George Whitfield, and William Carey just to name a few.[26]

It was in the school of prayer that Brainerd learned to pray, and it was in the school of prayer that his faith increased.

---

[26] As stated in the beginning paragraph of the section entitled, "The Theological Look," the excerpts for this chapter were taken from the following book: John Piper, *The Hidden Smile of God: The Fruit of*

The Personal Look: A Battle Fought Through Prayer

Recently, a close pastor friend of mine (Shane Hall) was diagnosed with cancer. This diagnosis would serve to place him, his wife, and his church in the school of prayer. Here is his story:

> I was diagnosed with stomach cancer in October 2014. By the time of the diagnosis, the cancer had metastasized, and the doctors informed me that the median life expectancy for my particular type of cancer was nine months. In circumstances like this, you realize that the Christian cliché that "God never puts more on you than you can handle" is without merit. Instead, the reality is that we often experience more than we can handle so that it might drive us, in absolute dependence, to our Lord and God.
>
> Through that diagnosis, God drove my wife and me to our knees in prayer. We had nowhere to turn but to turn to Him in faith. My wife and I prayed not knowing what the end game would be. We most definitely prayed for a complete and miraculous healing, yet we had to pray for something beyond the healing. We grabbed ahold of the promise in I Peter 1:6-9, "In this you greatly rejoice, even though now for a little while, if necessary, you have been distressed by various trials, so that the proof of your faith, being more precious than gold which is perishable, even though tested by fire, may be found to result in praise and

Affliction in the Lives of John Bunyan, William Cowper, and David Brainerd (Wheaton: Crossway Books, 2001).

glory and honor at the revelation of Jesus Christ; and though you have not seen Him, you love Him, and though you do not see Him now, but believe in Him, you greatly rejoice with joy inexpressible and full of glory, obtaining as the outcome of your faith the salvation of your souls." Our prayer was that God would refine our faith through the trial. Our prayer was that God would be glorified in the midst of our living and possibly even in the dying.

We thank God that at this point and time He has brought healing to my physical body. It was an answer to not only our prayers but also the prayers of countless others. But even if He had not brought the healing, we believe that He answered the prayer for refining—a refining of our faith, through the trial, that we pray resulted in praise and glory being given unto Him. In all things, He has been faithful.

Sadly, as this book was being prepared for publishing, Shane Hall succumbed to the cancer that he fought for over three years. He pastored and faithfully proclaimed the gospel until the end. Just like Brainerd, in the midst of the difficulties and struggles, Shane remained true to his calling. He too was driven by a desire to finish well. Also, like Brainerd, Shane had a remarkable prayer life. Now he worships the Lord in heaven without hindrance.

Practical Advice

1. Allow God to have His way with you through the adversity.

2. Pray for His will to be done.

3. Praise God in the midst of the adversity.

The Weapon of Prayer

2 Kings 18-21

Have you ever noticed that when you commit to prayer, every distraction seems to come against you? The distractions can be outward such as the dog barking, the baby crying, the kids fighting, or the phone ringing. However, the distractions can also be inward, such as a wandering mind, or unconfessed sin. Distractions should serve to remind us of the reality of spiritual warfare. Satan fears the power of a praying Christian. Therefore, he will attempt to do everything he can to keep you from prayer. In this section, I want to discuss "The Weapon of Prayer."

Hezekiah, son of Ahaz, succeeds him to the throne and is an exceptionally good king (2 Kings 18:3). There is a revival during his reign (vs. 4, 5). Hezekiah is able to overcome the Philistines, but Sennacherib, king of Assyria, invades Judah and threatens Jerusalem. Rabshakeh, the captain of Assyria, insults Hezekiah and attempts to frighten him.

The Biblical Look: The Praying King

E.M. Bounds referred to Hezekiah as "The Praying King." He further wrote, "The great religious reformation under King Hezekiah and the prophet Isaiah was thoroughly impregnated with prayer in its various stages."[27] I love the word picture: both men were full of prayer. And as a result, the movement itself was full of prayer — and God received all the glory.

First, I want to highlight the climate of Hezekiah's day. The nation of Israel had already gone into captivity at the hand of the Assyrians. At this point, Judah stood alone and was vulnerable to her enemies. This was at the beginning of the final 135 years before Judah went into captivity herself. The nation had drifted into idolatry and was in desperate need of spiritual reform.

Hezekiah arrived on the scene in the midst of such deplorable conditions. He was a good king who sought to honor God. He began his reign by "instituting sweeping religious reform." He immediately broke with Ahaz's Assyrian policy, perhaps because the Assyrians were facing some problems of their own. These difficulties were soon overcome, though, and Hezekiah was forced to pay Assyria tribute to stave off annihilation.[28] Here we find a good king

---

[27] E.M. Bounds, *Prayer and Praying Men* (Grand Rapids: Baker Book House, 1977), 54.

[28] Paul R. House, *The New American Commentary: 1, 2 Kings* (Nashville: B&H Publishing, 1995), 350.

seeking to rule in a very unstable environment. However, the grace of God carried him through.

<u>In 2 Kings 18:1-8, the author recorded the faithful character and **devotion** of Hezekiah</u>. Finally, there was a king who acted as he should. He removed the high places and all the images of false worship. Hezekiah desired to restore Jerusalem to the central place of worship.

However, the enemies of God had different plans. In 2 Kings 18:13-37, Sennacherib pushed back against Hezekiah's rebellious attitude and invaded the land. Given his desperate situation, Hezekiah attempted to make peace before the enemy reached Jerusalem. He did this via a letter to Sennacherib at Lachish. Sennacherib responded back by asking for a cluster of wealth. In a frantic attempt for peace, Hezekiah sought to raise the money. He raided Judah's treasury and stripped the temple of its gold. In spite of this, Sennacherib moved forward with his plan to attack Jerusalem.

<u>In 2 Kings 19:1-4, Hezekiah received wise, **discerning** counsel</u>. Hezekiah found out that the money he sent did not pacify Sennacherib, so he responded with mourning. This act further demonstrated Hezekiah's reliance upon the Lord. His counselors encouraged him to pray, which he was eager to do. Not only did Hezekiah pray, but he also sent his counselors to the prophet Isaiah to hear a word from the Lord. Through the prophet, God encouraged Hezekiah and promised destruction upon those who blaspheme His name.

In 2 Kings 19:8-13, God used threats of invasion to distract Sennacherib from invading Jerusalem. He received a report that Tirhakah of Egypt was marching out to fight him.

Therefore, instead of an actual invasion, Sennacherib once again chose to threaten Hezekiah. Just like Sennacherib, the enemy of the people of God (Satan) is always relentless in his attacks, and just like Satan, Sennacherib blasphemes the name of God.

Once again in 2 Kings 19:14-37, we see Hezekiah's **dedication**. After receiving the message from Sennacherib, Hezekiah turned to the Lord in prayer. In the midst of this seemingly impossible situation, Hezekiah clung to his hope in God. Through prayer, he asked God directly for His help. God answered the prayer of Hezekiah and promised to punish those who sought to oppress Judah. The mockery of Sennacherib had not gone unnoticed. The Assyrians would be punished. In the meantime, God promised to send them home by the route they came. They would reap what they had sown. In one single night, God killed 185,000 of their soldiers.

In 2 Kings 20, we see Hezekiah's **desire**. Hezekiah became sick and his time had come to die. He prayed for a recovery, and God heard his prayer. In this chapter, we also see Hezekiah's **disorder**. His heart became full of pride, which in turn led to prayerlessness. As a result, he permitted the ambassadors from Babylon to see his treasures.

In this account, we truly see that prayer is a weapon against our enemies. Hezekiah faced many challenges. There was the relentless assault from his enemies. There was also the challenge of personal illness. In both situations, Hezekiah responded in prayer, and on both occasions, God heard his prayers. The prayer of Hezekiah resulted in God destroying his enemies and healing his body. Prayer was not only a weapon for Hezekiah; prayer is also a weapon for all God's children. Praying men and women are the great need of our day. Perhaps E.M. Bounds stated it best when he wrote, "A breed of Christians is greatly needed who will seek tirelessly after God, who will give Him no rest, day and night, until He hearkens to their cry. The times demand praying men who are all athirst for God's glory, who are broad and unselfish in their desires, quenchless for God, who seek Him late and early, and who will give themselves no rest until the whole earth be filled with His glory."[29]

While the darkness glooms around us, while morality spirals downward, while addiction destroys lives and families, while divorce is common, and while depravity is paraded in the streets, let us use our mightiest weapon against darkness, PRAYER.

The Theological Look: The Most Valuable Resource

In this portion of the book, I will discuss the relationship between prayer and spiritual warfare. First, what is spiritual warfare? War is a state of conflict. "Spiritual" refers to the immaterial things that we cannot see, such as the human soul. Therefore, spiritual warfare is the state of conflict in the unseen world. Spiritual warfare began before mankind was even created. Lucifer, the archangel of God, sought to usurp the throne of God. God is sovereign, and Lucifer lusted after His sovereignty. Lucifer, along with a third of the angels, led a revolt in the heavens against God. God, being all-powerful, thrust Lucifer and the fallen angels (demons) to the earth. Now, the war that began in the cosmos is upon the earth.

---

[29] E.M. Bounds, *The Weapon of Prayer* (Grand Rapids: Baker Book House, 1931), 66.

When God created man, He placed him in the Garden.
God gave Adam authority over the Garden. However, there
came a warning. Adam and Eve were given access to the
fruit of the trees in the Garden, but they were commanded
not eat of the tree in the middle of the Garden (the tree
of knowledge of good and evil). They were told if they eat
of it they would surely die. Lucifer (Satan) continued his
war against God by attacking His creation. He tempted
Eve to eat from the very tree God had warned them not to
eat from. Eve, seeing that the tree was "good for food and
that it was pleasant to the eyes and a tree to be desired to
make one wise, ate of the fruit thereof," thereby succumbed
to the temptation of Satan. She then "gave also unto her
husband (Adam) with her, and he did eat" (Gen. 3:6).
Eve succumbed to temptation, but Adam willfully sinned.
This blatant act of rebellion is known as "The Fall." When
Adam fell, being the federal head of the human race, all of
humanity fell with him.

However, in Genesis 3:15, God promises to send one
born of the seed of the woman who would one day crush
the head of the serpent (Satan). In this verse, God said He
would put "enmity between you (talking to Satan) and the
woman; also between your offspring and her offspring."
This war declared by God includes all mankind. Therefore,
you are either fighting with God or against Him, depending
on your relationship with Christ. You see, in the fullness of
time, the Savior came forth, born of a virgin. At the cross,
Satan thought Christ had been defeated. But nothing could
be further from the truth. The cross was like the bruising
of Christ's heal because three days after His burial He rose
in victory. Christ's death and resurrection crushed the head
of the ancient serpent. Consequently, he has received a fatal
blow. Therefore, all of redeemed humanity has ultimate

victory over the devil through Christ. The words of Charles Spurgeon ring so true, "Satan is no longer the prince of God's people. His reigning power is gone. He may tempt, but he cannot compel. He may threaten, but he cannot subdue, for the crown is taken from his head, and the mighty are brought low."[30]

Even though Satan has ultimately been defeated, he still rages, seeking all whom he may devour. He is carrying on his battle on a large scale. He is a defeated, but very desperate foe. He is wise and extremely vicious. He would love nothing more than to destroy the lives of all of Christ's followers. We must not live in fear. Instead, we should take up our crosses as Christ did. In our daily battles against Satan, we must take up the weapon of prayer. In the words of William Gurnall, "God can overcome His enemies without help from anyone, but His saints cannot so much as defend the smallest outpost without the strong arm of the Lord."[31] Take up the weapon of prayer.

No matter how hard we try to resist, we will succumb to Satan's wicked devices if we fail in prayer. In the Garden of Gethsemane, Jesus told His disciples to stay awake and pray lest they fall into temptation. Jay Adams wrote, "Prayer is the means by which the Christian warrior calls on the Spirit for assistance. Your best intentions will come to nothing if you depend upon your weak self to win the battle."[32]

---

[30] Charles Spurgeon, *Spiritual Warfare in a Believer's Life* (Lynwood, WA: Emerald Book, 1993), 20.

[31] William Gurnall, *The Christian In Complete Armour: Volume 1* (Edinburgh: The Banner Of Truth Trust, 1964), 34.

[32] Jay Adams, *The War Within: A Biblical Strategy for Spiritual Warfare* (Eugene, OR: Harvest House Publishers, 1989), 87.

The great Puritan, John Owen, wrote, "Our Savior teaches us how to avoid entering into temptation: Watch and Pray."[33] First, to watch means to be on guard against. Consider your weaknesses and all the ways the enemy might seek to approach you. Second, pray. This is the most important duty of the Christian. Prayer is the means of drawing upon the strength of God; it is the very air of the Christian soldier.

The Apostle Paul taught the believers at Ephesus about the reality of spiritual warfare. He taught them how to be prepared and to fight well in 6:10-20. The unprepared believer is easy prey for the devices of the Devil. Our own strength will never be strong enough to resist Satan. However, just a little of God's strength is more than enough. Paul told the Ephesians to be "strong in the Lord" appropriating that the strength of God only comes through grace and prayer. One cannot possibly be clothed in the full armor of God without prayer. After all, the battle is spiritual. Therefore, it must be fought spiritually. Paul, at the conclusion of his instructions, writes, "Praying at all times in the spirit, with all prayer and supplication. To that end keep alert with all perseverance, making supplication for all the saints" (Eph. 6:18).

Prayer is a resource that believers have, and Satan does not possess. Prayer is our powerful weapon; it must not be neglected. We should never expect to overcome temptation if we fail to pray.

> To God your every need
> In instant prayer display

---

[33] John Owen, Richard Rushing, *Temptation: Resisted and Repulsed* (Carlisle, PA, Banner of Truth Trust, 2007), 18-19.

Pray always; pray and never faint
Pray! Without ceasing, pray.[34]

The Historical Look: A Preacher Combating Despondency

During his remarkable 38-year ministry, Charles Spurgeon was a seasoned veteran when it came to battling Satan. Spurgeon saw first-hand the power of Satan. Many in his congregation were kept in the bondage of sin, enslaved by the powers of their own lust. Bondage kept many from being influenced daily by the gospel. Therefore, their spiritual development was greatly anemic. This brought great discouragement and even depression to the life of Spurgeon.

Spurgeon once wrote, "I know Satan has used me, many times, when he wanted a sharp word to be said against somebody. 'Nobody,' says the devil, 'can hurt or grieve that person better than Mr. Spurgeon. Why, he loves him as his own soul. That's the man to give the unkindest cut of all, and he shall give it.' Then I am led, perhaps, to believe some wrong things against some precious child of God and afterward to speak of it. And then I grieve to think that I should have been so foolish as to lend my heart and tongue to the devil. Let us take heed lest we become instruments of Satan."[35]

Mr. Spurgeon spoke from his own experiences. Spurgeon believed he could not live without prayer. He also believed that neglected prayer was the source of all evil. Make no

[34] Albert Ernest Richardson, *The Kneeling Christian* (Alachua, Fla: Bridge Logos Foundation, 2007), 24.
[35] Spurgeon, 34.

mistake about it, if you neglect your prayer closet you will fail in your battle against sin.

Spurgeon knew first-hand the battle of adversity and spiritual warfare.

On October 19, 1856, he preached for the first time in the Music Hall of the Royal Surrey Gardens because his own church would not hold the people. The 10,000-seating capacity was far exceeded as the crowds pressed in. Someone shouted, "Fire!" and there was great panic in parts of the building. Seven people were killed in the stampede and scores were injured.

Spurgeon was 22 years old and was overcome by this calamity. He said later, "Perhaps never a soul went so near the burning furnace of insanity, and yet came away unharmed." But not all agreed he was unharmed. The specter weighed upon him for years, and one close friend and biographer said, "I cannot but think, from what I saw, that his comparatively early death might be in some measure due to the furnace of mental suffering he endured on and after that fearful night."

Spurgeon also knew the adversity of family pain. He had married Susannah Thompson on January 8 in the same year of the calamity at Surrey Gardens. His only two children, twin sons, were born the day after the calamity on October 20. Susannah was never able to have more children. In 1865 (nine years later), when she was 33 years old, she became a virtual invalid and seldom heard her husband preach for the next 27 years until his death. A rare cervical operation was attempted in 1869 by James Simpson, the father of modern gynecology, but to no avail (see note 36).

So, added to Spurgeon's other burdens was a sickly wife and the inability to have more children—though his own mother had given birth to seventeen children.

Spurgeon knew unbelievable physical suffering. He suffered from gout, rheumatism and Bright's disease (inflammation of the kidneys). His first attack of gout came in 1869 at the age of 35. It became progressively worse so that "approximately one-third of the last twenty-two years of his ministry was spent out of the Tabernacle pulpit, either suffering, or convalescing, or taking precautions against the return of illness." In a letter to a friend he wrote, "Lucian says, 'I thought a cobra had bitten me, and filled my veins with poison; but it was worse, — it was gout.' That was written from experience, I know." So, for over half his ministry, Spurgeon dealt with ever increasingly recurrent pain [such as in] his joints that cut him down from the pulpit and his labors again and again, until the diseases took his life at age 57 where he was recuperating in Mentone, France.

The final adversity I mention is the result of the others—Spurgeon's recurrent battles with depression. It is not easy to imagine the omnicompetent, eloquent, brilliant, full-of-energy Spurgeon weeping like a baby for no reason that he could think of. In 1858, at age 24 it happened for the first time. He said, "My spirits were sunken so low that I could weep by the hour like a child, and yet I knew not what I wept for."

He saw his depression as his "worst feature." "Despondency," he said, "is not a virtue; I believe it is a vice. I am heartily ashamed of myself for falling into it, but I am sure there is no remedy for it like a holy faith in God."[36]

In spite of all these sufferings and persecutions, Spurgeon endured to the end and was able to preach mightily until his last sermon at the Tabernacle on June 7, 1891. The weapon of prayer for Mr. Spurgeon was his most valuable weapon in his battle against adversity.

The Personal Look: A Life Saved

When I was a younger pastor, I was asked to visit a man whose wife and kids had left him due to his excessive drug abuse. When I arrived at his home, I knocked on the door. I was not surprised when no one answered. I decided to poke my head in the door and say, "HELLO." I could hear a faint voice in the back say, "Come on in." When I walked into the living room, I saw a truly pitiful sight. He was sitting there with a rubber hose wrapped around his arm and a needle full of dope on the coffee table. I could tell by the amount of dope in the syringe he was preparing to kill himself.

His eyes had lost their color. I only saw darkness in them. He was literally skin on bones. I could sense the presence of evil in the house. Satan wanted to kill this man and destroy his family in the process.

I started sharing the gospel with him. However, all he wanted to do was argue and make excuses. He blamed his wife for what he was about to do, which was to kill

[36] Piper, John. *Charles Spurgeon: Preaching Through Adversity*, www.desiringgod.org/messages/charles-spurgeon-preaching-through-adversity.

himself. After sharing the gospel, I then shared my personal testimony, hoping my own story of deliverance would encourage him to trust Christ. Once again, what I shared fell on deaf ears. I could tell he was getting irritated and wanted me to leave. I knew I was in a spiritual battle for this man's soul. I shared every evangelism outline I knew, and nothing seemed to work. Often, he would interrupt me mid-stream and not even allow me to finish. The darkness of his eyes seemed to penetrate through me. His language progressed in its vulgarity the longer we went. Satan and sin had a stronghold on him. But I was not going to give up that easily. I started talking with him about his family, hoping this would soften his heart, but to no avail. Actually, he became angrier, clinched his fist, and I prepared myself for defense.

I pulled out the small New Testament (with Psalms and Proverbs) from my back pocket. Then, I began to pray out loud for his salvation, and for his deliverance from addiction. I also prayed that the Spirit of the living God would be the only spirit present. I called on the name of Jesus, proclaiming the power of His blood to change lives and drive out evil. Still, in a state of prayer, I began to read Psalms 127-128 out loud. As I was praying, I began to hear a noise come from the man. It was not vulgarity or shots of anger, but it was crying. The man began to weep, confessing his sins while calling out on the name of Jesus. Suddenly, the presence of evil began to lift from the room, until it was gone altogether.

The man looked up at me, and the first time I saw his green eyes, the darkness was gone. He was now in his right mind. We hugged and wept together. Long story short, he got the help he needed, his wife and kids came back home, and the last I heard they were actively involved in church together.

I learned an invaluable lesson that day. I tried every evangelism strategy I had ever learned. I shared the three points of my testimony in five minutes like I was taught. But nothing I tried worked. It wasn't until I prayed and began to read from the Scriptures that evil felt the pressure to flee. God used prayer and His Word to break the heart of this hardened sinner. When Hezekiah prayed, God heard, and the evil was driven out. When Spurgeon prayed, God heard, and the evil was driven out. When I prayed, God heard, and the evil was driven out.

Application

1. Pray daily and read God's Word. Hold fast to trust in the promises of God.

2. Identify your weakness and keep your greatest distance from sin.

3. Memorize Scriptures that specifically deal with your greatest areas of weakness.

4. Enlist an accountability partner and give them permission to ask you the tough questions.

The Hope
of Prayer

Ezra 9-10; Neh. 1

Prayer and hope are two of the greatest needs in our day. We live in a prayerless society that has basically forgotten God. As a result, people are without hope. Suicide and school shootings have become the norm. People are addicted to antidepressant drugs at the highest level in our nation's history. However, in such a sad state of affairs, there is hope. Prayer offered in the name of Jesus provides such hope.

The Biblical Look: A Priest in Soul-Travail

Ezra, the Priest, ministered during a sad state of affairs. He had only been in Jerusalem a few days when the report came in about the sinful condition of the people of God. The people had failed to separate themselves from the people of that country. They were intermarrying with other nations, which was strictly prohibited by God. If that were not enough, they were adopting their pagan practices. By all appearances, the situation seemed hopeless. However, we must remember that there is always hope with prayer. Hope is not founded in the prayer itself, but to whom the prayer is being offered. God is omnipresent, and there is always hope when God is involved. Therefore, there is always hope in prayer.

Upon arriving in Jerusalem, Ezra found the people of God hopelessly paralyzed in their immorality. The people had prostituted themselves to pagan deities. They had intermarried and began to establish families. The religious life of the people was literally nonexistent, except for their pagan practices. Everything seemed to indicate that the people were too far gone for reformation or revival.

However, Ezra did not run from the situation. He cared enough to do something. He saw the situation and realized just how serious it was. He was honest about the situation, and he did not minimize the reality of the condition. The situation was sad. Ezra was grieved so much that he tore his garments, plucked out his hair and beard, and sat down appalled (Ezr. 9:3).

In this state of soul-travail, he gave himself intensely and persistently to prayer. He confessed the sins of the people and prayed to God for His pardoning mercy (Ezr. 9:6-15). Prayer was the only means to move God, and a supernatural move of God was their only hope. Ezra prayed, and God moved. Remember, prayer is never hopeless when you are praying to God because God can do all things. As a result of Ezra praying, reformation and revival were brought to

Israel. American believers would do well to learn this lesson from Ezra.

Nehemiah was a contemporary of Ezra, and he too was a man of prayer. When he heard the distressing news that the walls were still down in Jerusalem and the gates were not hung, he also broke down in afflicting prayers to God. Being deeply distressed by the information, he mourned and wept before God. These are the types of prayers that move the hand of God; the prayers offered up from the depths of our spiritual man in brokenness. In his prayer, he adores God, beseeches the mercy of God, and confesses the sins of the nation. God granted Nehemiah favor in the heart of the Persian ruler and allowed Nehemiah to travel to Jerusalem. As Ezra worked on the spiritual condition of the people, Nehemiah worked on the physical structure of the city itself.

After arriving in Jerusalem, Nehemiah faced resistance that grew moment-by-moment in its intensity. But in everything, Nehemiah prayed. No task was too menial or too great. He prayed over every situation. Even after the walls were completed, those in opposition did not relent from their attacks. Nehemiah, even as they opposed him, persistently and prevailingly gave himself to prayer.

Nehemiah eventually traveled back to Persia and, in his absence, the people once again reverted back to their pagan customs. This is the result of prayer being overlooked. Once again, Nehemiah returned to find evil among the people of God. Fortunately, for the people of God, they had two leaders that were committed to prayer: Ezra, and Nehemiah. Both men knew there is always hope in prayer when you are praying to God.

In the words of E.M. Bounds, "Prayer helps to build churches and to erect the walls of houses of worship. Prayer defeats the opponents of those who are prosecuting God's enterprises. Prayer favorably touches the minds even of those not connected with the Church and moves them toward Christian matters. Prayer helps mightily in all matters concerning God's causes and wonderfully aids and encourages the hearts of those who have His work in hand in this world." I would also add, there is always hope in prayer when praying to God. Therefore, there is no such thing as a truly hopeless situation.

The Theological Look: The Importance of Persistence

Jesus told His disciples that "men ought to always pray and not lose heart" (Luke 18:1). The context in which Christ spoke this was the parable of the persistent widow. To pray and not lose heart is to pray with hope. As stated above, there is no such thing as a hopeless situation when God is involved. Therefore, prayer offered up to God should always be filled with hope. There are two things we must guard against: laziness and losing heart regarding prayer. The widow kept coming to the unjust judge. She knew her persistence would eventually pay off. She was filled with hope.

Our God is not an unjust judge. To the contrary, He is loving and kind. If an unjust judge, who does not fear God, knows how to give into persistence and hope, how much more does a loving heavenly Father. Of course, all things prayed for should be in line with His sovereign will. When we pray according to the Word of God, our prayers should be persistent and full of hope.

Hope in prayer allows us to hold on and not give up. Remember, "The effective, fervent prayer of a righteous man accomplishes much." E.M. Bounds refers to this as "wrestling in prayer." Furthermore, he wrote, "Nothing distinguishes the children of God so clearly and strongly as prayer. It is the one infallible marks and test of being a Christian. Christian people are prayerful, not worldly-minded. Prayer must be habitual, but much more than habit. It is a duty, yet one which rises far above, and goes beyond the ordinary implications of terms. It is the expression of a relation to God, a yearning for Divine communion."[37] I would further add, prayer is an exercise of faith, which in turn instills hope.

Prayer is about molding our hearts to trust in God. The more we pray in hope, the greater hope we will have. Prayer is not meant to change God. Prayer changes us. We live in the days of the blessed hope (Christ's imminent return), and we are to reflect that hope while here on earth. There is always hope in prayer when it is aligned with the Word of God and offered to God. After all, He can do all things.

The widow in our parable had a prayerful resilience; she would not be denied. She clung to her faith because her heart was filled with hope. The same is true for Ezra and Nehemiah. Both men looked upon what seemed to be a hopeless situation, but they knew there was hope as long as God is on His throne. So, they prayed, and God heard. Your situation may seem hopeless, but don't lose heart. There is always hope in prayer when it is being offered to an omnipotent God. Therefore, "Always pray and don't lose heart."

---

[37] E.M. Bounds, *The Necessity Of Prayer* (Grand Rapids: Baker Book House, 1976), 64.

The Historical Look: A Persistent Hope

George Müller was a native German (a Prussian). He was born in Kroppenstedt on September 27, 1805 and lived almost the entire nineteenth century. He died on March 10, 1898, at the age of 92. He saw the great awakening of 1859, which he said, "led to the conversion of hundreds of thousands." He did follow-up work for D. L. Moody, preached for Charles Spurgeon, and inspired the missionary faith of Hudson Taylor.

Each day as George Müller walked the streets, he saw children everywhere who were orphans. They lived on the streets or in state-run poorhouses, where they were mistreated. George felt God calling him to open an orphanage to take care of the children.

George prayed, asking God to provide a building, people to oversee it, furniture, and money for food and clothing. God answered his prayers. The needs of the orphanage were met each day. Sometimes a wealthy person would send a large amount of money, or a child would give a small amount received as a gift or for doing chores. Many times, food, supplies or money came at the last minute, but God always provided without George telling anyone about his needs. He just prayed and waited on God.

More than 10,000 children lived in the orphanage over the years. When each child became old enough to live on his own, George would pray with him and put a Bible in his right hand and a coin in his left. He explained to the young person that if he held onto what was in his right hand, God would always make sure there was something in his left hand as well. The following is one example of Mr. Müller's hope in prayer.

> "The children are dressed and ready for school. But there is no food for them to eat," the housemother of the orphanage informed George Müller. George asked her to take the 300 children into the dining room and have them sit at the tables. He thanked God for the food and waited. George knew God would provide food for the children as he always did. Within minutes, a baker knocked on the door. "Mr. Müller," he said, "last night I could not sleep. Somehow I knew that you would need bread this morning. I got up and baked three batches for you. I will bring it in."

It has been more than 165 years since George Müller took in his first orphan. His vision continues today as Christians around the world are inspired by his faith to depend on God to meet their needs and the needs of helpless children.[38] There is always hope in prayer when it's being offered up to God. When God is involved, there is no such thing as a truly hopeless situation.

The Personal Look: A Family Bound by Prayer

The first church I pastored was a rural, country church 15 miles from the closest town, and the town did not even have a red light. There, I ministered to a family that had

---

[38] *George Mueller, Orphanages Built By Prayer*, www.christianity.com/church/church-history/church-history-for-kids/george-mueller-orphanages-built-by-prayer-11634869.html

recently lost one of their teenage daughters to cancer. It was truly a sad situation. They had watched their daughter fight and then eventually dwindle down to skin and bones. It was heart-wrenching.

Not long after this, another one of their teenage daughters was in a terrible automobile accident. Her injuries were life-threatening, and she had to be airlifted to Tulsa, Oklahoma. Her brain began to swell, and she was on life support. When I received the news, the situation was described to me as "hopeless." They had already started calling in family to prepare them for the worst.

As soon as I received the news, I drove to Tulsa. I couldn't believe it! This family just watched one daughter be eaten away by cancer and now this. However, I chose to cling to hope and not give into despair. When I walked into the ICU, I saw her bruised and battered body lying there. Tubes seemed to protrude from everywhere. The sight was quite overwhelming, but I also knew there was hope in prayer. Not because there was something special about my prayer, but the special person to whom my prayer was offered— God. There is no such thing as a hopeless situation when God is involved. Together with the family, I read Scripture over her and prayed fervently for her healing. God gave me confidence that day that He was going to heal her, and that is exactly what happened. They were able to get the swelling in her brain under control, and a few days later she woke up from the coma. Today she is married and raising her beautiful children.

We know that not all prayer results in physical healing. But there are times when God chooses to use our prayers to accomplish His divine purposes. Therefore, there is always hope in prayer.

Application

1. Make a list of three people who seem to be in a hopeless situation and pray for them.

2. Many groan over the moral decline of our nation. Instead of complaining, choose to pray fervently for God to send spiritual awakening.

3. Pray for many sick and dying churches to experience genuine revival.

The Sustaining Power of Prayer

Daniel 6

Early on in my Christian journey, I would often see believers go through devastating events, such as the loss of a child, or terrible bouts of chemotherapy. I observed these faithful believers, even though understandably heartbroken, remaining steadfast in their faith. I can remember thinking, "How can they have peace in the midst of horrific suffering?" Yes, it was because of their saving relationship with Jesus Christ, but there was something else; they were men and women of prayer.

The Biblical Look: The Witness of Unswerving Prayer

It was a notable experience in the life of Daniel when he was ordered by the king, while in Babylon, not to pray or petition God for thirty days. If he failed to obey the king's edict, the penalty would be the lions' den. However, Daniel paid no attention to the edict. The Scripture records, "When Daniel knew that the document had been signed, he went to his house where he had his windows in his upper chamber open toward Jerusalem. He got down on his knees three times a day and prayed and gave thanks before his God, as he had done previously" (Dan. 6:10). Obviously, kneeling in prayer was the regular habit of Daniel. God sustained Daniel and answered his prayer by sending His angels to shut the mouths of the lions.[39]

It would have been very easy for Daniel to compromise his convictions. After all, he was a captive in a foreign land. However, Daniel did not cave to compromise at any moment. He was a man of prayer and prayer sustained him. Surrounded by pagan deities, he never forgot God. Daniel's life is a great example of the power of prayer to sustain us, even in dire situations. He was living in a pagan land, and the environment was anything but godly.

Daniel's ministry began when God gave the Babylonians victory over Judah. He, along with other Hebrew young men, was taken into exile. Upon arrival, Nebuchadnezzar certainly sought to indoctrinate them. When Daniel and his friends were presented with the king's prescribed diet, they asked to be excused. Obviously, Daniel feared God more than the pagan king. Fearing that his own life would be taken if Daniel's health suffered, Daniel's overseer begged him to eat the king's food. However, Daniel trusted God and stood his ground. Even though prayer is not mentioned in this passage, we have already established that Daniel was a man of consistent prayer. Daniel refused to compromise because prayer sustained him. While others

---

[39] E.M. Bounds, *Praying And Praying Men* (Grand Rapids: Baker Book House, 1977), 89.

caved to compromise, Daniel remained steadfast and resolute (1:8-16). Daniel was a man of principle, and he had his priorities in the right place. Godly principles and godly priorities are the results of a life sustained by prayer. Prayerlessness leads to misplaced priorities, which in time gives way to compromise.

God rewarded Daniel and his friends for their resolute faith by blessing them with exceptional wisdom. Soon upon Daniel's arrival in Babylon, Nebuchadnezzar had a dream. He asked his pagan magicians to interpret the dream, but they could not. Furious at their failure to produce, the king ordered that all the wise men of Babylon be killed (2:1-23). Daniel and his friends were numbered among the wise men; this meant certain death for them. However, God gave Daniel insight into the king's dream. Once again, we see the sustaining power of prayer. The wisdom Daniel gained through prayer provided him with the ability to discern God's voice and interpret the king's dream, which ultimately saved his life and the lives of his friends. Daniel gives full credit to God for his ability to interpret the dream (2:24-28). Here we see that Daniel was a man of perception. He had the spiritual discernment to interpret the dream because he was a man of prayer. Prayerfulness gave him the perception he needed to see things from God's perspective.

Perhaps, the greatest display of the sustaining power of prayer was seen in Daniel's unwillingness to bow to the king's edict. Eventually, the Medo-Persians invaded Babylon, and the Babylonian king Belshazzar was killed. Darius the Mede became Babylon's new king (5:30-31). Daniel found favor in the eyes of Darius and became one of his top advisors (6:1-3). However, this made some of the other leaders very angry. Therefore, they conspired against Daniel and sought a way to have him executed. In a blatant act of deception, they convinced the king to establish an edict that barred all prayer to anyone except the king (6:1-9).

Daniel was not moved by fear, but devotion to God. Therefore, he prayed as usual. Ultimately, Daniel's conspirators exposed him to the king (6:10-13). Immediately, the king regretted his decision and tried to release Daniel, but to no avail. After his failed attempts to free Daniel, the king had Daniel thrown into the lions' den. The courage Daniel manifested was the outflow of his personal prayer life. Prayer's sustaining power resulted in Daniel's faithfulness when many others would have compromised. Those who often give in to compromise are often weak in prayer. Strong praying results in strong living. The sustaining power of prayer filled Daniel with a spiritual passion for God.

Early the next day, Darius, the anxious king, ran to the mouth of the lions' den. Upon arrival, he found Daniel alive and well. Daniel praised God for protecting him. God had sent an angel to shut the mouths of the lions (6:19-23). Subsequently, Daniel's accusers were thrown into the lions' den, and the king issued a decree that Daniel's God be honored throughout the empire (6:24-27).

Of course, this is an amazing account of God's faithfulness. However, do not miss the importance of prayer. Daniel was a normal man, not a superhuman, who stood strong in the face of compromise because he believed in the sustaining power of prayer. We too can stand strong in the face of compromise if we believe in the sustaining power of prayer.

Prayer can sustain you to stand upon Biblical principles, establish godly priorities, gain spiritual perception, and look in the face of lions with courageous passion.

The Theological Look: The Gift of Prayer

Prayer has everything to do with God. It was God's business to sustain Daniel in the midst of compromise, but God invited Daniel to be a part of it through prayer. Prayer is an invitation from God to be a part of what He is doing. Those who fail to pray miss out on the greatest blessings.

However, there is a greater point that needs to be expressed. Men and women who are saved by the grace of God are called to be active in God's work. Therefore, we are obligated to pray. It is the grace of God that compels us to pray. Grace motivates me to stand strong in the face of compromise, but I will never be able to stand strong when I am weak in prayer. Prayer positions me to walk in the fullness of God's sustaining grace. I am not saying that prayer is a work to perform in order to obtain grace. If this were the case, it would not be grace, but obligation. To the contrary, the desire for prayer itself is an act of grace wrought in us by holy God. If God, by His Spirit, did not compel us to pray, we would never pray. Therefore, when I submit to the Spirit's leading and pray, I experience God's sustaining grace. E.M. Bounds wrote, "God is vitally concerned that men should pray. God does His best work for the world through prayer. God's greatest glory and man's highest good are secured by prayer."[40]

---

[40] E.M. Bounds, *The Reality Of Prayer* (Grand Rapids: Baker Book House, 1924), 35.

God encourages us to pray, not because He needs prayer, but because we need prayer. Without prayer, we are like a sheet of paper driven by the wind, prone to compromise with every gentle breeze. Therefore, let us pray, not only because there is certainty of an answer when we pray according to the will of God, but we also need to be sustained. If we are men and women of prayer, we will stand in grace like giant oaks when the winds of compromise blow our way.

Remember, it is God who gave us prayer. He gave us prayer as a gift, and it serves a vital purpose. One such purpose is the power to sustain us in the face of compromise. Paul's own understanding of the power of prayer to sustain is expressed in his second letter to the Thessalonians. He wrote, "Finally, brothers, pray for us, that the word of the Lord may speed ahead and be honored, as happened among you, and that we may be delivered from wicked and evil men. For not all have faith. But the Lord is faithful. He will establish you and guard you against the evil one" (2 Thess. 3:1-3). Paul requests prayer, but he also realizes that God will use prayer to establish and guard the believers in Thessalonica against compromise. The sustaining power of prayer is a gift from God to the believer, and we are obligated to use it. Thus, prayer is both a gift and an obligation. Use it wisely.

The Historical Look: The Praying Martyr

The Early Church was hated by the society and government of the Roman Empire for various reasons, such as the refusal of Christians to sacrifice to the gods. The Empire went through many phases of demanding that the Christians sacrifice—which meant denying their faith—or be killed. The earliest attacks claimed the lives of many of the apostles.

This story, from around 160 AD, is of the martyrdom of Polycarp, the Bishop of the church in Smyrna, a city in Asia Minor (modern Izmir in Turkey) devoted to Roman worship. The account is in the form of a letter from eye-witnesses to other churches in the area. It is the earliest chronicle of a martyrdom outside the New Testament.

Polycarp, the venerable bishop of Smyrna, hearing that persons were seeking for him, escaped but was discovered by a child. After feasting, the guards apprehended him. He desired an hour in prayer. When allowed, he prayed with such fervency, that his guards repented that they had been instrumental in taking him. He was, however, carried before the proconsul, and condemned to be burnt in the marketplace.

The proconsul then urged him, saying, "Swear and I will release thee—reproach Christ."

Polycarp answered, "Eighty and six years I have served Him, and He never once wronged me; how then shall I blaspheme my King, who hath saved me?" The proconsul once again declared, "I have wild animals here," the Proconsul said. "I will throw you to them if you do not repent." "Call them," Polycarp replied. "It is unthinkable for me to repent from what is good to turn to what is evil. I will be glad though to be changed from evil to righteousness." "If you despise the animals, I will have you burned." "You threaten me with fire which burns for an hour, and is then extinguished, but you know nothing of the fire of the coming judgment and eternal punishment, reserved for the ungodly. Why are you waiting? Bring on whatever you want."

At the stake to which he was only tied, but not nailed, as usual, he assured them he should stand immovable. From there he prayed, "O Lord God Almighty, the Father of your beloved and blessed Son Jesus Christ, by whom we have received the knowledge of you, the God of angels, powers and every creature, and of all the righteous who live before you, I give you thanks that you count me worthy to be numbered among your martyrs, sharing the cup of Christ and the resurrection to eternal life, both of soul and body, through the immortality of the Holy Spirit. May I be received this day as an acceptable sacrifice, as you, the true God, have predestined, revealed to me, and now fulfilled. I praise you for all these things, I bless you and glorify you, along with the everlasting Jesus Christ, your beloved Son. To you, with him, through the Holy Ghost, be glory both now and forever. Amen."[41]

The flames, on their kindling the wood, encircled his body, like an arch, without touching him; and the executioner, on seeing this, was ordered to pierce him with a sword, when so great quantity of blood flowed out as extinguished the fire. But his body at the instigation of the enemies of the Gospel, especially Jews, was ordered to be consumed in the pile, and the request of friends, who wished to give it a Christian burial, rejected. They nevertheless collected his bones and as much of his remains as possible and caused them to be decently buried.[42]

---

[41] *The Martyrdom of Polycarp*. Translated by J.B. Lightfoot. www.christianhistoryinstitute.org/study/module/polycarp.

[42] John Foxe, *Foxes Book Of Martyrs* (Peabody, Ma: Hendrick-

Polycarp stood faithfully as a martyr being sustained by the power of prayer.

The Personal Look: A Continued Reliance Upon Prayer

Recently, one of our staff members was diagnosed with cancer. I asked her to share her story of God's faithfulness to sustain her through prayer.

> Prayer is sometimes referred to as life-changing encounters with God. This truth has become evident in my life throughout the years. I am amazed at the peace 'talking to God' brings. Talking to God is what I often say to teachers, parents, and children, never realizing how much this communication with God would bring peace during some of the most difficult days I would face.
>
> In October of 2014, my world was changed as I heard a physician confirm that I have a life-threatening illness, cancer, one I am all too familiar with, knowing that this dreaded disease had taken its toll on many of my family members, including my parents.
>
> Reading His word brings comfort, truth, and peace in the midst of the unknown future. As I began the journey of treatment, many nights and days all I could do was talk with God, knowing He was holding me and providing for my every need. Vision was not something that

son Publishers, 2004), 14.

came easy, due to the chemotherapy treatments. I began listening to His word instead of reading.

One particular passage found in Daniel was a reminder of God's faithfulness. Daniel's faith was tested as he was put into the lions' den, yet, his faith did not wavier and mine cannot either. In Matthew 6:8 He reminds me "...for your Father knows what you need before you ask Him." Many times, I cry out to God for physical help knowing that His plan for me is perfect and He has not, nor will ever leave me alone on the journey of life. This truth has been one of the verses along with prayer that sustains me daily.

Hearing my husband and others offering fervent, consistent prayers for healing brings comfort knowing God is listening to all prayers. Reading the Scriptures over and over again as I struggle with the discomfort and constant reminders that my battle is not over, reminds me that God is the Creator, and He is providing for my health and future. What a joy it is to know that He is always listening to my prayers and holding me tightly in His hands.

Many years ago, a pastor challenged us to find a verse that we can use as a life verse. "Trust in the Lord with all your heart, and do not lean on your own understanding. In all your ways acknowledge Him, and He will make straight your paths" (Proverbs 3:5-6). These verses reflect my desire to serve and pray to Him constantly. God is ever present, and He will never leave me. He will simply hold me and mold me for His purpose.

Her story continues as her battle with cancer is not over. However, God continues to strengthen and sustain her through her prayers and the prayers of others for her.

Practical Steps

1. Pray even when you don't feel like it.

2. Dwell on the things you are truly thankful for.

3. Ask God to help you learn from Him during this time in your life.

The Mission of Prayer

Acts 16:11-34

The missionary heart of God is without question. Since the beginning, God has been seeking to redeem lost humanity back to Himself. His missionary heart does not only include the nation of Israel but all the nations of the world. One day in heaven, circled around the throne, there will be worshipers from every tribe, tongue, and language. God wants to use you and your prayers to accomplish this great task.

The Biblical Look: The Praying Apostle

The Apostle Paul, above anything else, was a man of prayer. Throughout his ministry, his days were spent in prayer. His ministry career actually began with prayer. In Acts 9, we have the account of Paul's conversion. Just before his conversion on the Damascus road, he was a part of the brutal killing of one of the Lord's disciples, Stephen. I'm sure the unnecessary killing of Stephen lingered in his mind. After receiving letters that authorized him to throw Christians in jail, Paul set out for Damascus.

While on his way, Paul experienced a miraculous event, his conversion. According to Scripture, a bright light shown all around, while the voice of Jesus spoke from heaven. The brightness of the light was the glory of the resurrected Christ. When He spoke, He spoke as one with authority. The intense light caused Paul to fall to the ground. In response to Paul's question, "Who are you, Lord?", Jesus reveals Himself. It was there, on that lonely road, that Paul's life was forever changed.

When Paul arose from the ground, he could not see. He had been struck with blindness. Paul spent some time in Damascus recovering from seeing the glory of the Lord, which resulted in blindness. For several days, he sat contemplating what had occurred and certainly during that time God was preparing him for ministry. During that time a disciple named Ananias received a vision from the Lord. Ananias was ready to obey. Notice, what God told him, "Rise and go to the street called Straight, and at the house of Judas look for a man of Tarsus named, Saul, for behold, he is praying" (Acts 9:11). Thus, we see that the missionary work of Paul began with prayer.

Furthermore, his first missionary journey, along with Barnabas, was birthed in prayer. The Scriptures state, "While they (the church of Antioch) were worshiping the Lord and fasting, the Holy Spirit said, 'Set apart for me Barnabas and Saul for work to which I have called them.'

Then after fasting and praying they laid their hands on them and sent them off" (Acts 13:2-3). Both men learned this practice, and everywhere they went to establish churches they did the same. E.M. Bounds wrote, "Praying made up the substance, the bone, the marrow, and the very being of their religious life."[43] They understood that the success of their mission hinged on their willingness to pray.

The Theological Look: A Desire to See the Lost Be Saved

We learn from the above account that God uses prayer to open hearts. I have already stated in this book that God is sovereign, and He can do whatever He wants all by Himself. He does not need you or me. He is totally self-sufficient. However, God wants to use us and has chosen to use us as a means of accomplishing His redemptive end. Ultimately, God's redemptive purposes will be fulfilled either with or without you. If you choose not to pray, then He will use someone else, and you will miss out on the blessing and the eternal reward God wants to give you.

Therefore, I ought to be praying for the hearts of lost men and women to be opened to the gospel. Specifically, I should call them out by name. Currently, I have a prayer list of several people I'm praying for. I am asking God to open their hearts so that they might be saved. God does not need me to twist His arm, He is eager to save, but He does need me to pray for them. My prayer for the lost ought to be fervent, persistent, and specific. Along with praying for their hearts to be opened, I should pray for God to use me as the means of accomplishing this end. Often, we pray for

---

[43] E.M. Bounds, *Prayer And Praying Men* (Grand Rapids: Baker Book House, 1977), 123.

God to send someone else, but in reality, He has placed that person on your heart because He wants to use you beyond your prayers. Incredibly enough, God uses our prayers to open hearts to receive the gospel.

The Historical Look: The Birth of a Missions Movement

Five Williams College students met in the summer of 1806, in a grove of trees near the Hoosack River, then known as Sloan's Meadow, and debated the theology of missionary service. Their meeting was suddenly interrupted by a thunderstorm and the students, Samuel J. Mills, James Richards, Francis L. Robbins, Harvey Loomis, and Byram Green, took shelter under a haystack until the sky cleared. "The brevity of the shower, the strangeness of the place of refuge, and the peculiarity of their topic of prayer and conference all took hold of their imaginations and their memories."

In 1808, the Haystack Prayer group and other Williams students began a group called "The Brethren." This group was organized to "effect, in the persons of its members, a mission to" those who were not Christians. In 1812, the American Board of Commissioners for Foreign Missions (ABCFM) sent its first missionaries to the Indian subcontinent.

Samuel Mills became the Haystack person with the greatest influence on the modern missions movement. He played a role in the founding of the American Bible Society and the United Foreign Missionary Society.

Through the work of Byram Green, a monument was erected in Mission Park in Williamstown, MA, in 1867 to honor the five men involved in the Haystack prayer meeting. In 1906, a gathering took place in Mission Park at Williams College in Massachusetts to remember the prayer meeting of one hundred years before. In the summer of 2006, those committed to missions celebrated the 200th anniversary of the Haystack prayer meeting.[44]

Think about it, a foreign mission movement that began with a group of guys praying under a haystack. In its first fifty years, the ABCFM sent out over 1250 missionaries.

The Personal Look: A Convicted Heart

I can remember one summer's day in 2001 when God convicted me greatly over my lack of personal evangelism. I was serving as a youth pastor at the time and was also attending classes at Southwestern Baptist Theological Seminary. The day started just like any others, I had my quiet time, went to the office for a few hours, and then jumped in my truck and started the thirty-minute drive to the seminary.

On the short journey toward the seminary, God began to convict me deeply. I knew that I had not been sharing the gospel as I should have. At that moment, God broke my heart once again for the lost. I began praying and calling out to God to give me someone to witness to along the way. Every broken-down car on the side of the interstate caught my attention. I thought, "If I see someone there, I'm going to stop, help them and share my faith." However, car after car was unoccupied.

---

[44] Global Ministries. *The History of the Haystack Prayer Meeting,* www.globalministries.org/the_history_of_the_ haystack_pray_10_10_2014_112

I continued to pray for God to give me someone to witness to. Soon I had to exit off of the interstate, which is about two miles from the seminary. After exiting, I pulled up to a red light and noticed a man standing on the corner with a sign that simply read "I NEED HELP." Immediately, I pulled over and asked the man how I could help him. He stated that he needed a ride across town to get to the homeless shelter before dark. So I loaded him up and together we started our journey across town. I spent the next forty-five minutes sharing the gospel with him. Before leaving him at the shelter, he prayed to receive Jesus as his personal Lord and Savior.

This truly is the mission of prayer: to see people saved for the glory of God.

Practical Advice

1. Pray daily for God to give you someone to witness to.

2. Pray daily for God to make you aware of it when He does.

3. Pray daily for God to give you the courage to carry it through.

The Peace
of Prayer

1 Samuel 1:1-19

The Biblical Look: A Distressed Woman

In the story described in this Scripture, we have a situation of desperation brought on by barrenness. However, the situation is made worse as the direct result of polygamy. The sorrow is expressed through Hannah, the barren wife of Elkanah. She was dearly loved by her husband, but the jealousy of the embittered wife, Peninnah, weighed heavily upon her. Her barrenness and the constant attacks of her rival produced in her a very sorrowful spirit.

The desperation of her situation is further highlighted by the grammatical structure of the narrative. In verse 5 it states, "...the Lord had closed her womb," then in verse 6: "...her rival provoked her." This resulted in her being "...

grievously irritated." The pattern is repeated, verse 6: "...
the Lord had closed her womb;" then verse 7: "...she used
to provoke her;" and the end of verse 7 states, "Therefore,
Hannah wept and would not eat." This repeated structure
paints a very sorrowful situation.

However, in the midst of her struggle, Hannah took refuge
in the Lord. Often, the purpose of affliction is to draw us
closer to the Lord. This was the case with Hannah. While
everyone else was enjoying a celebratory time, she took the
time to pray at the temple to the Lord (v.9). The temple
mentioned was not a permanent structure, but a large tent.
It was here that her agony found words in the form of a
vow. She was so fully absorbed in her prayer that she did
not even notice Eli. She forgot herself, her surroundings,
and was lost in prayer. She knew that God was her only
hope.

The making of the vow was her way of acknowledging that
the child would be a gift from God. The statement, "...and
no razor shall touch his head," seems to suggest this was a
life-long Nazirite vow. Hannah voluntarily offered up this
vow on behalf of her son. I believe it is important to note
that this is descriptive of what God placed upon Hannah's
heart. This is not to be interpreted as prescriptive for every
barren mother who prays for a child. However, all of our
children are to be consecrated to the Lord.

The narrator prepares his readers for the apostasy of the
priesthood in chapter two by contrasting the spiritual
sensitivity of Hannah against the lack of spiritual
discernment found in Eli. Eli rebuked her because
he assumed she was drunk. However, after seeing the
genuineness of her faith, Eli sought to encourage her.

There is a contrast presented here that can be overlooked if we are not careful. First, we see a distraught Hannah—unwilling to eat—who went to pray, but the Hannah who returned was different. She was at peace. Though her outward circumstances had not changed, she was joyous, hopeful, and at peace.

I want to highlight several noteworthy aspects of her prayer: it was personal (v.7); it was desperate (v.10); it was specific (v.10); it was honorable (v.11); it was continual (v.12); and it was sincere (v. 12, 15). As a result of praying, she was encouraged and at peace.

The Theological Look: A Perspective of Peace

John MacArthur wrote, "Peace is commonly defined as the sense of calm, tranquility, quietness, bliss, contentment, and well-being that we feel when everything is going the way we'd like it to go."[45] However, MacArthur believes this definition is incomplete and I agree. For example, these characteristics could be produced by many outward influences such as pills or alcohol. This is not the kind of calm contentment that we learn from the Bible.

Biblical peace cannot be produced by any outside influences at all. Manufactured peace will never last. However, the peace that God gives is not subject to outside influences; it's an eternal peace. It is a peace that comes from knowing God. In my own experience, it's an attitude of the heart to trust God no matter the circumstances or consequences. Most of the world's population is unaware of this peace. The reason for this is that this peace can only be found

---

[45] John MacArthur, *Anxious For Nothing: God's Cure for the Cares of Your Soul* (Colorado Springs: Victor Publishing, 2006), 103.

in a personal relationship with Jesus Christ. Jesus Himself stated, "Peace I leave with you; My peace I give to you. Not as the world gives do I give to you. Let not your hearts be troubled, neither let them be afraid" (John 14:27).

Peace itself is an attribute of God. God is a God of peace. God knows all things, sees all things and controls all things. He knows the end from the beginning. Therefore, He sits upon His throne in perfect, calm contentment. This is the very peace He gives us when we trust Him and pray to Him. Unquestionably, this is the peace Hannah had when she rose up from prayer. Amazingly enough, peace is a gift, not an experience that one must work for. Peace is not an event, a temporary emotion based upon pleasant circumstances. To the contrary, it's a way of life, a lasting state of mind which affects the heart. Peace is a gift from God that is given at the moment of salvation. It is a resource always at the believer's disposal. It is a well with no bottom, a cloud that is never dry. Without a doubt, it is the believer's possession and the believer's prosperity.

However, this does not negate the fact that peace must be guarded. We have an enemy who loves nothing more than to rob Christians of their peace. For this reason, the Apostle Paul wrote, "Rejoice in the Lord always; again I will say, rejoice. Let your reasonableness be known to everyone. The Lord is at hand; do not be anxious about anything, but in everything by prayer and supplication with thanksgiving let your requests be made known to God. And the peace of God, which surpasses all understanding, will guard your hearts and your minds in Christ Jesus" (Phil. 4:4-7). Notice, that Paul writes, '...let your requests be made known to God." This is prayer. When we pray, the peace of God will guard our hearts and minds. Without a doubt, this is good news.

Furthermore, Paul went on to write, "Finally, brothers, whatever is true, whatever is honorable, whatever is just, whatever is pure, whatever is lovely, whatever is commendable, if there is any excellence, if there is anything worthy of praise, think about these things. What you have learned and received and heard and seen in me—practice these things, and the God of peace will be with you" (Phil. 4:8-9). Once again, Paul mentions peace. Therefore, the believer has the responsibility of guarding peace through prayer and dwelling upon things that are worthy of praise. Someone may say, "There is nothing praiseworthy in my life." Let's look again at the characteristics of the things that are praiseworthy: whatever is true; whatever is honorable; whatever is just; whatever is pure; whatever is lovely; whatever is commendable. All of the above characteristics point to God. You may think you have nothing praiseworthy in your life right now, but if you have God, you have everything. Stop focusing on the seeming hopelessness of your situation and start focusing on God. As we guard peace through prayer and godly meditation, peace, in turn, guards our hearts.

The Historical Look: The Praying Hymn Writer

The following excerpt was taken from the book *Then Sings My Soul* by Robert J. Morgan.

When the great Chicago fire consumed the Windy City in 1871, Horatio G. Spafford, an attorney heavily invested in real estate, lost a fortune. About that time, his only son, age

4, succumbed to scarlet fever. Horatio drowned his grief in work, pouring himself into rebuilding the city and assisting the 100,000 who had been left homeless.

In November of 1873, he decided to take his wife and daughters to Europe. Horatio was close to D.L. Moody and Ira Sankey, and he wanted to visit their evangelistic meetings in England, then enjoy a vacation.

When an urgent matter detained Horatio in New York, he decided to send his wife, Anna, and their four daughters on ahead. During the small hours of November 22, 1873, as the ship glided over smooth seas, the passengers were jolted from their bunks. The ship had collided with an iron sailing vessel, and water poured in like Niagara. The ship tilted dangerously. Screams, prayers, and oaths merged into a nightmare of unmeasured terror. Passengers clung to posts, tumbled through darkness and were swept away by powerful currents of the icy ocean. Within two hours, the mighty ship vanished beneath the waters. The 226 fatalities included Horatio's four daughters. Mrs. Spafford was found nearly unconscious, clinging to a piece of wreckage. When the 47 survivors landed in Cardiff, Wales, she cabled her husband: "Saved Alone."

Horatio immediately booked passage to join his wife. En route, on a cold December night, the captain called him aside and said, "I believe we are now passing over the place where the ship went down." Spafford went to his cabin but found it hard to sleep. He said to himself, "It is well; the will of God be done." He later wrote his famous hymn based upon those words.[46]

---

[46] Robert Morgan, *The Sings My Soul* (Nashville: Thomas Nelson Publishers, 2003), 185.

When peace like a river, attendeth my way,
When sorrow like sea billows roll;
Whatever my lot, Thou has taught me to say,
"It is well, it is well, with my soul."

Horatio truly understood and experienced the peace of prayer.

The Personal Look: A Prognosis of Peace

The former Children's Minister of our church and his wife (Charles and Stephanie Scheffe) just went through a very difficult time in their lives. I asked them to briefly share their story.

> There are some days that you never forget in your life. July 24th, 2016, was one of those days. My wife and I were headed to an ultrasound. We had our only daughter who was six with us, and we were excited to find out the sex of the baby. After what seemed like an hour the doctor came in and began talking to us about a potential problem and the need to run an additional test. As he started detailing a prognosis of death for the baby—we were shell-shocked.
>
> With the exception of talking to our parents, we really did not say much for the first two weeks as we attempted to unravel what had been shared with us. And we began to pray. We prayed that the tests would come back negative and that the doctors would have an answer. We prayed for miraculous healing. We slowly began

to invite others to pray with us. Finally, we shared with our church family, and together we spent the next three months of the pregnancy praying and believing in God for a miracle.

In the midst of the praying, we noticed a change. Not a change in the baby, nor a change in the prognosis, but in us. I also noticed the change in others that had been praying with us. Finally, my mom, just a few weeks before Caroline was born, put words to what the rest of us had begun to sense and understand. One day after our Sunday meal, my mom said, "I think I will be OK. No matter what happens, God has given me a peace that I know I can survive this."

That was exactly what God had been doing in my life, and my wife's too. But that is a scary thing to say. And it is a scary thing to feel. At first, I thought it was just a defeatist mindset. But as I watched our little girl being born and realized the number of surgeries and difficult life she would have faced, I thanked God for His decision that I could have never made. She lived for only a few short minutes before God took her home to heaven. God had given us peace; peace that He was still God, and that He was still in control and peace that everything, even through the hurt and the pain, would still be oaky. God used our prayers to provide us supernatural peace.

Practical Steps

1. Meditate on the attributes of God.

2. Meditate on the names of God.

3. Memorize the promises of God.

The Disciples' Prayer

Matt. 6:1-14

Priorities are so easy to misplace. To be honest, our prayer lives are not immune to misplaced priorities. As a matter of fact, if we were all honest with ourselves, we would say that more often than not our prayers lack godly priority. In this passage, Jesus is going to help us establish godly priorities as it relates to our prayer lives.

The Biblical Look: A Model for Prayer

In this passage, Jesus draws a contrast between true and false prayer. The Pharisees, known for their false righteousness, were guilty of making prayer a spectacle, a sideshow demonstration of their hypocrisy. As a result, their prayers were defective, and the content was selfish. Prayer, for them, had become ritualized, nothing more than a formality to be followed. Jewish liturgy supplied prescribed prayers that were recited several times daily. They had prescribed prayers for every occasion. This type of endless repetition makes prayer obsolete.

Furthermore, they tended towards long, drawn-out prayers. Often, prayers were offered up in public places such as busy streets corners or town squares. Here, they would pray standing with hands stretched out, palms held upward, and heads bowed. Because of their hypocrisy, their prayers were being offered to people and not to God.

It should not be a surprise to any of us that we too could fall into the same hypocritical practices if our spiritual lives are left unchecked. Jesus combats the false practices of the Pharisees by giving instruction for genuine prayer. First, He states that it should be "in secret." Jesus Himself went away often to pray. Making a habit of praying in secret will guard our hearts against hypocrisy. This is not a rebuke against all public praying, Jesus Himself prayed publically (Jn. 6:11; 11:41-42). But it is a rebuke against praying publically to put one's righteousness on display. Without a doubt, if a person does not pray privately, then he or she has no business praying publically. Jesus also promises that if God is the true audience of our prayer, then He will give reward from heaven. As stated above, Jesus warns against meaningless repetition. He desires for our prayers to be sincere and from the heart. God knows what we need before we ask, but He still wants us to ask. He desires to hear and commune with us in prayer.

Jesus not only gives instruction for genuine prayer, but He also provides a model for His disciples to follow regarding genuine prayer. Verses 9-15 are commonly known as the "Lord's Prayer," however, Jesus is not praying. He is teaching His disciples how to pray. Therefore, a more accurate title is the "Disciples' Prayer." Or, as others have suggested, "The Model Prayer."

Before entering into the contents of the prayer, a few introductory remarks will serve us well. First, Jesus does not give His disciples this prayer to pray it over and over again. Certainly, there is nothing wrong with praying this prayer verbatim if it is offered from a pure heart and not out of formalism. Jesus said, "Pray then like this," not "pray this." Therefore, this prayer serves as a model. Secondly, let's look at the characteristics of this prayer. "The prayer consists of three parts: an invocation ('Our Father who art in heaven'), six petitions and a conclusion ('For Yours is the kingdom,' etc.). The priority of the prayer is in harmony with the fact that, according to both the Old and New Testament, the glory of God is important above everything else, the first three petitions have reference to the Father's name, kingdom, and will. Human needs—bread, pardon for sin and victory over the evil one—take the second place."[47]

This prayer consists of fewer than seventy words, but it opens our eyes to the mind of God. My goal here is not to break down each phrase of each verse, but to give an overview. John MacArthur in his commentary on Matthew offers a helpful summary:

When outlined from the perspective of our relationship to God, we see:

---

[47] William Hendrickson, *New Testament Commentary: Matthew* (Grand Rapids: Baker Academic, 1973), 325.

Our Father showing the father child relationship; **hallowed be Thy name**, the Divine and the worshiper; **Thy kingdom come**, the Sovereign and the subject; **Thy will be done**, the Master and the servant; **give us this day our daily bread**, the Benefactor and the beneficiary; **forgive us our debts**, the Savior and the sinner; and **do not lead us into temptation**, the Guide and the pilgrim.

From the perspective of the attitude and spirit of prayer, **Our** reflects unselfishness; **Father** reflects family devotion; **hallowed be Thy name**, reverence; **Thy kingdom come**, loyalty; **Thy will be done**, submission; **give us this day our daily bread**, dependence; **forgive us our debts**, penitence; **do not lead us into temptation**, humility; **Thine is the Kingdom**, triumph; **and the glory**, exultation; and **forever**, hope.[48]

Therefore, we learn from this verse that "prayer is not trying to get God to agree with us or to provide for our selfish desires. Prayer is affirming God's sovereignty, righteousness, and majesty and seeking to conform our desires and our purposes to His will and glory."[49] Prayer is a means by which we express our total dependence upon God.

---

[48] John MacArthur, *The MacArthur New Testament Commentary: Matthew 1-7* (Chicago: Moody Publishers, 1985), 374.
[49] Ibid., 375.

The Theological Look: The Right Priority

We learn from this prayer that true prayer focuses and centers on God's glory and not human need. This is not to say that praying for human need is unimportant, but it is not to be the priority. The glory of God is always the primary issue. Yes, we pray to lay claim to the promises of God and to demonstrate our dependence on Him for all human need, but it's not about making demands of Him. Instead, prayer is about acknowledging the sovereignty of God and expressing a desire to see His glory as a result of obeying His will. In other words, our prayers are not to be man-centered, but God-centered. Clearly, we learn from this prayer that God is passionate about His own glory. Therefore, a passion to hallow God's name ought to be the driving force behind the prayers we pray.

When we read or pray this prayer, we ought to do it with a gospel focus. The only way to say "Our Father" is to know His Son (Jesus) personally. Furthermore, to truly "hallow" God's name (honor) a person must trust in the finished work of Christ (Christ's death, burial, and resurrection). Gospel intent is clearly in view when Christ teaches His disciples to pray "Your kingdom come." Graeme Goldsworthy has written, "Two things are inevitably linked with the coming kingdom: the salvation of people of God, and the judgment of all who reject the kingdom. To pray 'Your kingdom come,' then, expresses an identification of the petitioner with the purpose of God in the gospel. We are asserting and, at the same time, requesting that this great saving goal of God will come to pass."[50] Also, when we pray "Your will be done on earth as it is in heaven,"

---

[50] Graeme Goldsworthy, *Prayer and the Knowledge of God: What the Whole Bible Teaches* (Downers Grove: IVP Books, 2003), 93.

we are acknowledging the reality of two different realms. Therefore, we are to pray for the realm of man (earth) to reflect and be impacted by the realm of God (heaven). "It is a longing for the day promised by God through His prophets in the Old Testament. That day is the Day of the Lord when God finally acts to bring about the new heaven and the new earth."[51]

However, there is a "now" but "not yet" aspect of the kingdom reflected here. For example, the kingdom of God has come already in the person of Christ. Christ is the embodiment of the total rule of God, and He is the King who reigns over that kingdom. Therefore, in one sense the kingdom of God is in every believer, and in another sense, every believer is a part of the kingdom of God. The kingdom is the rule and reign of God on earth and Christ rules and reigns in the heart of every true believer. But in another sense, the kingdom of God is future. The kingdom grows and expands as the gospel is preached throughout the world. One day it will culminate with a new heaven and a new earth.

A whole lot more could be said theologically about this prayer. However, my goal in this section is to identify the priority of a gospel-focused prayer life.

The Historical Look: A Transformed Orator

Prayer is about positioning ourselves to be the mouthpiece of God. In the fourteenth century, a young man by the name of John Tauler was born in Strasbourg. Very little is known about his early life. By 1314, John was a novice monk in the Strasbourg monastery.

---

[51] Ibid., 95.

Later in life at the age of fifty, he had an experience that changed his life. He was a popular preacher with the usual ability to persuade congregations. People traveled from great distances to hear him preach. The story is told that on one occasion Nicolas of Basel traveled some 150 miles to hear him preach. After listening to Tauler list twenty-four steps on how a person becomes holy, Nicolas took notes on the message and in a later conference with Tauler read the notes back to the preacher. Nicolas told Tauler he ought to practice what he preaches. He also told him that he lacked power in the pulpit. After this conversation, Tauler stopped preaching for two years and spent time in meditation and prayer. Through this event, he experienced a personal renewal.

Before his personal revival, he was a popular preacher. After his renewal, he became God's spokesman. Before his renewal/revival, people responded to him as an orator. After his renewal/revival, they responded to him in deep conviction of sin. As the Holy Spirit worked through his prayers and preaching, entire communities experienced revival.[52]

Once Tauler aligned his prayer with God's agenda, revival broke out in many hard to reach areas. His personal legacy went on to impact the Reformers after him. The lessoned to be learned is simple: God uses people who align their prayers with His agenda and not their own.

---

[52] The historical account of John Tauler was taken from the following resource. Malcolm McDow & Alvin Reed, *Firefall: How God Has Shaped History Through Revivals* (Nashville: B&H Publishing, 1997), 121.

The Personal Look: A Shift in Viewpoint

I have asked one of my staff members to share a personal testimony about redirecting priorities in prayer. He wrote the following:

> I was working a job at which my predecessor hired me and would be my supervisor for the first two years. This arrangement was discussed during the interview process, and I was in agreement with it. When the two-year period passed, my boss came to me and said that he would be taking a new role within the organization, but that he also planned to maintain his leadership in the area that I was originally hired to do. Over time, my attitude went from frustrated and disappointed to angry and resentful. During that time, I prayed that God would remove this person to get him "out of my way" so that I could do the job that God had called me there to do. It seemed the more I prayed, the more things stayed the same and the more resentful I became.
>
> One day I was reading in Ephesians 1, and God really spoke to me through a particular verse. The Apostle Paul said, "I pray that the perception of your mind may be enlightened so you may know what is the hope of His calling, what are the glorious riches of His inheritance among the saints..." (Ephesians 1:18). Through that passage, I saw that my attitude and my thoughts toward that person and toward God

were sinful. God convicted me of praying to invoke my will and not His will.

As I redirected my prayers, I began to ask God to use me to make a difference, either in my current job or in another place. It did not happen overnight, but my heart and my attitude changed from that point on. I began trying my best to honor God in the job I was doing instead of in the job I thought I should be doing. After a few years, God opened a door for me to relocate and serve in a position for which I believe I was made. Over time, I have realized that in my years of frustration and disappointment God was preparing me for the job, which I now do and love. It wasn't until my prayers became more God-focused and less self-focused that God began to release me from that job and prepare me for the next stage in my life.

Practical Steps

1. Commit to daily prayer.

2. Commit to godly priorities in prayer.

3. Commit to gospel-focused and filtered prayers.

Conclusion

As we have seen, prayer is the strongest weapon at the Christian's disposal. It offers far more than any self-help book, counseling session, or prescription drug ever could. We have seen that prayer can alter our lives, intercede for us, teach us, protect us, give us hope, sustain us, be instrumental in the salvation of souls, give us peace, and shift our perspective.

Prayer truly is a gift from God. It is a privilege for those who know God through a relationship with Jesus Christ. We ought to be grateful that he has given it to us, and as with any gift, put it to good use. We ought to be a people of prayer—a people who do not pray out of ritual or tradition, but out of total surrender to and reliance upon our Lord.

I hope this book has been an encouragement to you. I hope it has changed the way you think about prayer. I also hope you will take these principles with you and not put them down with the book. If you commit to becoming a person of prayer, the Lord will certainly use you in a mighty way. He will take your weaknesses and make them strengths in the Kingdom of God.

Finally, I would like to leave you with this: keep praying. If you have been praying to see a loved one come to know the Lord and it feels like it will never happen, keep praying. If you have been praying for clarity in a difficult situation and things only seem to be getting more difficult, keep praying. If you have been praying to see revival come and things only seem to be getting worse, keep praying. In the words of our Lord, "And I tell you, ask, and it will be given to you; seek, and you will find; knock, and it will be opened to you. For everyone who asks receives, and the one who seeks finds, and to the one who knocks it will be opened" (Luke 11:9-10).

My Prayer For You

Heavenly Father, I pray for Your blessing upon the readers of this book. I pray that by Your grace they will grow in wisdom, knowledge, and understanding. Help them to be totally reliant upon You no matter what they may be going through. Bless them and keep them. Cause Your face to shine upon them. I pray that in all their ways they will acknowledge You and that You will make their paths straight. Above all, help them to be men and women of prayer.

Bibliography

Adams, Jay. *The War Within: A Biblical Strategy for Spiritual Warfare.* Eugene, OR: Harvest House Publishers, 1989.

Bounds, E.M. *Prayer and Praying Men.* Grand Rapids: Baker Book House, 1977.

———. *The Necessity of Prayer.* Grand Rapids: Baker Book House, 1976.

———. *The Possibilities of Prayer.* Grand Rapids: Baker Book House, 1979.

———. *The Reality of Prayer.* Grand Rapids: Baker Book House, 1924.

———. *The Weapon of Prayer.* Grand Rapids: Baker Book House, 1931.

Enns, Peter. *The NIV Application Commentary: Exodus.* Grand Rapids: Zondervan, 2000.

Foxe, John. *Foxes Book of Martyrs.* Peabody, MA: Hendrickson Publishers, 2004.

George Mueller, Orphanages Built By Prayer, www.christianity. com/church/church-history/church-history-for-kids/ george-mueller-orphanages-built-by-prayer-11634869. html (accessed March 30, 2018).

Global Ministries. *The History of the Haystack Prayer Meeting*, www.globalministries.org/the_history_of_the_haystack_pray_10_10_2014_112 (accessed March 30, 2018).

Goldsworthy, Graeme. *Prayer and the Knowledge of God: What the Whole Bible Teaches.* Downers Grove: IVP Books, 2003.

Gurnall, William. *The Christian In Complete Armour: Volume 1.* Edinburgh: The Banner of Truth Trust, 1964.

Hamilton, Victor. *The New International Commentary on the Old Testament: The Book of Genesis, Chapters 1-17.* Grand Rapids: William B. Eerdmans Publishing Co, 1990.

Hendrickson, William. *New Testament Commentary: Matthew.* Grand Rapids: Baker Academic, 1973.

Hendrickson, William and Simon J. Kistenmaker. *New Testament Commentary: Thessalonians, the Pastorals, and Hebrews.* Grand Rapids: Baker Academic, 1984.

House, Paul R. *The New American Commentary: 1, 2 Kings.* Nashville: B&H Publishing, 1995.

Lightfoot, J.B. *The Martyrdom of Polycarp.* Translated by J.B. Lightfoot. Abridged and modernized by Stephen Tomkins. Edited and prepared for the web by Dan Graves, www.christianhistoryinstitute.org/study/module/polycarp (accessed March 30, 2018).

MacArthur, John. *Anxious for Nothing: God's Cure for the Cares of Your Soul.* Colorado Springs: Victor Publishing, 2006.

———. *The MacArthur New Testament Commentary: Matthew 1-7.* Chicago: Moody Publishers, 1985.

McCartney, Dan G., *Baker Exegetical Commentary on The New Testament: James.* Grand Rapids: Baker Academic, 2009.

McDow, Malcolm and Alvin Reed. *Firefall: How God Has Shaped History Through Revivals.* Nashville: B&H Publishing, 1997.

McGraw, Francis. *Praying Hyde.* Minneapolis: Bethany Fellowship, 1970.

Morgan, Robert. *The Sings My Soul.* Nashville: Thomas Nelson Publishers, 2003.

Owen, John and Richard Rushing. *Temptation: Resisted and Repulsed.* Carlisle, PA: Banner of Truth Trust, 2007.

Packer, J.I. *Evangelism and The Sovereignty of God.* Downers Grove: IVP Books, 1961.

Piper, John. *Charles Spurgeon: Preaching Through Adversity*, www.desiringgod.org/messages/charles-spurgeon-preaching-through-adversity (accessed March 30, 2018).

———. *The Hidden Smile of God: The Fruit of Affliction in the Lives of John Bunyan, William Cowper, and David Brainerd.* Wheaton: Crossway Books, 2001.

Richardson, Albert Ernest. *The Kneeling Christian.* Alachua, Fla: Bridges Logos Foundation, 2007.

Spurgeon, Charles. *Spiritual Warfare in a Believer's Life.* Lynwood, WA: Emerald Book, 1993.

———. *The Prayers of Christ.* Peabody, MA: Hendrickson Publishers, 2014.

Other Books by Blake Gideon

Identity – Living Your Life with Influential Purpose

I believe the first step for any Christian is to know who they are in Christ. If this first step is missed or perhaps later forgotten, it can lead to a life of continual frustration, disappointment, and even depression.

Every human being on the face of the earth has an established identity – and that means you. I am not talking about your name, social security number, or even your fingerprint; I'm talking about the way you see yourself and the words you speak to yourself. Because of the sin of mankind, we as humans tend to compare ourselves to others and speak self-defeating words in our mind.

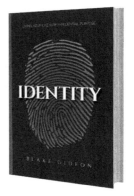

But I have great news for you: your internal negative dialogue can change! And this is what this book is all about.

Unvarnished Truth

What is Truth? A lot of people have asked that question through the ages. Unfortunately, our own opinions or desires often obscure the truth. For many, truth can become whatever we want to believe.

In much the same way as a person strips away layers of old paint or varnish to get the original beauty of a priceless antique, this book seeks to remove all the layers of lies and opinions that clog our culture, to get to the unvarnished truth of what really matters. Through this process, we'll see that the truth in Christ becomes our greatest story.

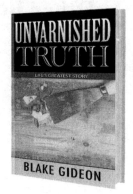

It is time to rediscover the unvarnished truth about God and accept Jesus' challenge to share that truth with others.

These and other books by Dr. Gideon can be purchased from his website: engagingthemind.org or from your favorite bookstore or online bookseller.